Meditations on the Lower Tantras

MEDITATIONS ON THE LOWER TANTRAS

from the collected works of the previous Dalai Lamas

Compiled and edited by
GLENN H. MULLIN

Assistant Editor
MICHAEL RICHARDS

The texts of this volume were translated by teams of Westerners working in consultation with authoritative Tibetan scholars, as credited at the end of each item.

LIBRARY OF TIBETAN WORKS & ARCHIVES

First Edition 1983
This Edition 1997

ISBN: 81-86470-13-1

Published by the Library of Tibetan Works & Archives, Dharamsala, H.P. and printed at Indraprastha Press (CBT), Nehru House, New Delhi.

CONTENTS

CONTENTS

PUBLISHER'S NOTE

The recent decades have seen an increasing maturity in the Buddhist centers in the West that are rooted in the Tibetan tradition. Many high lamas regularly tour the West to give teaching and initiations. The LTWA, being in communication with many of these centers, has had numerous inquiries concerning the practices of the various initiations received. As most of these initiations are open to the general public, the majority of them belong to the Lower Tantras. Thus it seemed useful to bring out a small handbook of the more common systems given.

In addition, there is also an increasing interest in Tibetan art and iconography. The Tibetan meditation manuals on the tantric systems throws a great deal of light on the symbolic forms and the essential characteristics of the deities meditated upon. These manuals also show how the individual tantric systems were integrated into the lives of the practicing community.

The major meditational deities of Tibet are, of course, the same as those of Buddhist India, being based on the Indian Buddhist Tantras. Thus this collection may prove of interest also to students of Indian and Asian art with roots in the tantras.

Gyatso Tsering,
Director, LTWA

EDITOR'S PREFACE

Tibetan Buddhism in practice represents the union of the Sutra and Vajra Vehicles taught by Buddha, or the exoteric and esoteric teachings. Moreover, all sects of Tibetan Buddhism agree that the Sutrayana methods should be mastered as a preliminary to application of the tantric techniques of the Vajrayana.

The dividing line between the Sutrayana and Vajrayana is initiation, or the receiving of the empowerment ceremony. In chapter one of the present volume the Seventh Dalai Lama describes how the mind must be cultivated before approaching the gateway to initiation. Most of the qualities that he refers to and the meditations that he suggests as prerequisites to receiving initiation have their basis in the Sutrayana trainings. Experience gained in the Sutrayana practices thus ripens the disciple for the tantras.

Initiation is given into one of four levels of the tantras. The first three of these are often referred to in Tibetan literature simply as "The Lower Tantras." (Tib. Og-mai-gyu). Above these are the sets of Highest Yoga Tantras (Tib. La-me-gyu) such as Kalachakra, Heruka and so forth. Each of the four categories of the Tantras has a large number of deities belonging to it, each deity symbolizing a complete yogic path to enlightenment.

Practice of the Lower Tantras involves two principal phases: the yoga of symbols and the yoga without symbols. The texts of this collection are concerned primarily with the former of these. Here the intellectualism of the Sutras melts and reappears as a vast array of symbols moulding and transforming within our mind's eye, a transformation that we become a part of; and through sharing in the mystical nature of the transformation, we ourselves arise as the deity to perform the mantric recitation that releases a wave of enlightened energy.

There are many ways to approach a study of the lower tantras. One such approach is by means of the category of literature known as *Ngak-kyi-sa-lam*, or "Stages and Paths of the Mantra Vehicle." Another popular category of literature on the subject is the *Gyu-de-nam-shak*, or "The Foundations of the Tantras" Both of the above deal with the tantras in a philosophical or technical manner, breaking down the elements of the yogas involved and relating them to stages in practice, etc. A number of texts of this nature are available in English translation.

The present collections makes no attempt to deal with the philosophical aspects of the Lower Tantras. Rather, its aim is simply to present a range of meditation manuals from the first stage of these systems. It should be noted here that most practitioners of the Highest Tantras also practice the Lower Tantras either from time to time or as a lifetime daily meditational endeavor. The First Dalai Lama, for example, a renowned practitioner of the Kalachakra Tantra, was even more famous for his applications to the Tara and Amitayus systems. Almost every Tibetan yogi today practices a daily *sadhana* of one or more of the Lower Tantra deities dealt with within the covers of this book.

The collected works of most Tibetan lamas are adorned by a type of literature called *Lha Drub*, or "Deity Accomplishment"; *Yidam Drub-khor*, or "Concerning the Meditational Deity Practices"; and also *Drub-thab-Kun-du*, or "Collection of Sadhanas." These deal with the various meditations related to the four (or six) tantra categories. It is from such sources in the *Collected Works* of the previous Dalai Lamas that we have drawn our materials.

Most of the Dalai Lamas (His Holiness the present Dalai Lama being fourteenth) have written extensively on the various Buddhist tantric lineages popular in their own times. Much of this literature deals with the Highest Yoga Tantras; yet there is also considerable attention given to the practices of the Lower Tantras. Texts of this nature can range in length from a few pages to several hundred folios. With the hope of presenting an introduction to a wide number of deities we have chosen from the shorter works of each system, the emphasis being to present a typical daily meditational practice for each. A number of the texts also deal with how the mantra of the deity is used for making retreats, special purposes such as health and longevity and for occasional practices such as fasting, etc. The aim with each is to show how the Lower Tantras are used in the life of an ordinary practitioner. There are many types of meditations and rituals associated with each system; our approach has been to select the fundamental "Self-identification" (Tib. dak-kye) or "Meditation and Mantra" (Tib.gom-de) category of text. These deal directly with spiritual rather than the magical usages of the tantra and thus more simply reveal the essential nature of the deity as a meditational device.

Tibetan sects are more houses of transmission of lineages than they are institutions, and a great deal of sharing of lineages occurs. Consequently even though, for example, the Amitayus practice in part one of Chapter Two is of the Kargyu tradition, having been brought to Tibet by Milarepa's disciple Rechungpa in the late eleventh century, the system nonetheless is practiced by Tibetans of all sects.

All Tibetan traditions teach more or less the identical deity—yoga systems; the main difference centers around which of the various methods are emphasized. In our selection we have tried to incorporate those deity practices of Lower Tantra that are common to all sects, rather than dealing with less common forms.

The Tibetan tantras have received criticism and their validity as Buddhist lineages has been questioned. In the traditional Tibetan view, the lineages of the various deities of the Buddhist tantras were taught in secret by Buddha, passed in secret for a thousand years in India and then, when the time was ripe, were propagated more openly. As Buddhism was carried from India to Tibet between the seventh and twelfth centuries, the tantric lineages came with it. These were practiced with great enthusiasm from that time onward. The larger deity manuals often include prayers to the Guru lineage of the system being used, giving the names of each successive master in the line of transmission.

A second reason for the attack on the tantric systems is the sexual and violent language characteristic of the Highest Yoga Tantras. Although the Dalai Lamas have written extensively on the Highest Tantras, none of these works are included in the present volume, which deals with "Meditations on the Lower Tantras." The language of the Lower Tantras is definitely more tame. The only work involving any sexual imagery is the Vajrasattva sadhana of Chapter six, and this only because the Vajrasattva system has a stronger connection with the upper tantras.

Manuals on the processes of transformation and creative imagination, such as those of this volume, sometimes read more like mystical theaters than anything else, and readers unfamiliar with literature of this genre should perhaps treat it as such. More familiar readers may find counterparts to their own practices in some of the works. Also, as many Tibetan Lamas are teaching and giving initiation in the west these days, perhaps some students of Tibetan Buddhism will find practices for which they have the initiation but no practice manual. with this in mind, the texts are selected with the hope of providing practices that are standard to most systems and do not involve any special Guru lineage visualizations.

CHAPTER ONE

The Preliminaries of Initiation

by the

SEVENTH DALAI LAMA (1708-1757)

The Preliminaries of Initiation

by the

SEVENTH DALAI LAMA (1708-1757)

The highest of all paths taught by Buddha Shakyamuni is the secret Vajrayana, the path of the *Guhyamantra* taught in the form of the mighty Vajradhara. Yet one cannot enter into this vehicle of practice without first acquiring the empowerments that ripen one's body, speech and mind for tantric practice; or the initiations or blessings that give birth to various abilities, such as the ability to generate qualities as of yet undeveloped, the ability to increase whatever qualities one may have, and so forth.

A teacher who wishes to lead fortunate trainees through the meditations and scriptural transmissions of this Secret Path should be qualified by an understanding and depth of experience that accords with the views of the great tantric treatises. His ornament should be the jewel of having received the appropriate lineage transmissions in accordance with clear explanations from qualified masters and yogis. He should not lead the disciple in accordance with personal fancy but should guide him through all phases of empowerment and tantric meditation precisely as outlined in the traditional scriptures. Without distractions or mental wanderings, at the time of the actual empowerment ceremony he should thoroughly perform the generation of the vision of himself as the Deity of the mandala and the generation of the external mandala. The disciple may then wash himself, enter the mandala, and offer the flower. Visualizing the Guru as being inseparably one in nature and appearance with the Deity of the mandala, he should make him an imaginary offering of all valuable things in this world, such as his own and others' bodies, possessions and so forth, as well as all goodness of the past, present and future.

The most important precept for the Guru is found in the words of the incomparable Atisha:

> When giving spiritual advice to others,
> Have the altruistic mind of compassion.

That is, the teachers' prerequisite for teaching Dharma is to abandon all superficial thoughts, such as personal gain or fame, and to generate the sublime thought to benefit others.

The disciple's basis is given in a Sutra:

> Listening correctly gives knowledge of all dharmas;
> Listening correctly leads away from evil;
> Listening correctly brings freedom from harmful forces;
> Listening correctly results in nirvana.

The Sutra continues:

"O son of noble family, if one listens well, wisdom will arise. If one has wisdom, mental distortion will subside. When one has no mental distortion, Mara the Evil One is unable to gain victory."

As this passage suggests, if one dedicates energy to listening to the holy Dharma one will gain an understanding of the spiritual qualities to be cultivated and negative qualities overcome. Once this knowledge is generated one can begin to work on engendering perfections such as ethical discipline, samadhi and wisdom.

In this context the master Vira wrote:

> The highest spiritual aspirant
> Constantly listens to a few teachings.
> By continually collecting the few,
> Before long much is acquired.
> What happens to a vessel
> Placed outside in the rain
> Of tiny droplets of water
> Falling in an unbroken stream?
> From this clear illustration
> We can, O King, clearly see
> That one should constantly delight
> In listening to the holy Dharma.

One should therefore listen most enthusiastically to every line of Dharma possible, so that before long one will go to the other side of listening and knowledge.

The value of striving to hear the holy Dharma was stated by the great Lama Tzong Khapa:

> When listening to the sacred Dharma
> Consider yourself most fortunate.
> With a face radiant with joy
> And a smile exuding delight,
> Listen with a mind free of the three pot-like faults.

Whenever one attends a Dharma discourse or empowerment ceremony, one should first generate a joyous mind by contemplating the beneficial effects of hearing Dharma. The external sign of this contemplation is a face radiant with joy, a smile exuding delight and a manner of reverence.

This is the basis for listening with a mind free of the three faults, which are likened to three pots—an overturned pot, a pot contaminated with poison, and a pot with a hole in its base.

Letting the mind wander deludedly to external objects while attending a Dharma event is like pouring water into an overturned pot. Listening to Dharma while holding impure thoughts such as having no faith in the Guru, seeing faults in him, having jealousy or pride, wanting to gain transient happiness or worldly occult power and so forth, is like pouring water into a poisoned pot. Finally, if the student has an attentive mind and a creative motivation but does not attempt to retain what he has learned, teaching him is like pouring water into a pot with a hole in its base. Guard yourself against these three faulty attitudes if you would gain maximum benefits from attending a discourse on the mystic Dharma.

One should listen to Dharma teachings in order to be able to gain a state of realization that would contribute to freeing living beings from the ocean of misery. The motivation should be to gain the wisdom of Buddha, not wealth or prestige; to triumph over the enemy which is one's own delusion, not to be able to win in debate and argumentation; to respectfully master the essence of Dharma, not to steal an occult trick from the spiritual friend. This is how the Sutras instruct us to listen.

If we were to abbreviate from the Sutras and Tantras all the advice on how to listen to Dharma, the most essential precept would be to maintain the thought: "By all means possible I must strive to achieve the precious stage of perfect Buddhahood, the peerless awakening, the highest spiritual attainment, in order to benefit the limitless sentient being who are as vast in number as the extent of space. Solely to actualize this goal am I listening to this perfect discourse on the excellent Dharma."

In the case of a tantric empowerment or initiation one replaces the last line with, "Solely to actualize this goal am I attending this event of the Vajrayana Dharma, the Secret Path." This thought establishes the perfect motivation, first of the four perfect conditions for tantric practice.

Secondly we must create the perfect environment. Visualize that the place of the tantric event is the inconceivable celestial mansion produced from the spontaneously appearing wisdom of the meditational deity. Seated upon a throne upheld by eight fearless lions at the center of this fantastic palace is one's tantric master, inseparably one in nature and appearance with the meditational deity.

The third perfect condition is perfect company. Visualize that you and all others present are the five meditational Buddhas, the various Bodhisattvas and so forth.

Lastly we should try to experience perfect activity. Visualize that the master's voice resounds like the melodious sound of Brahma, sending out clouds of sounds to the various disciples in accordance with their individual spiritual needs.

The general attitude toward the subject one is listening to, the holy Dharma, is described in *Selected Sayings of Buddha:*[1]

The wise people of this world
Make firm their faith and wisdom,
For these are supreme jewels
Outshining all others.

Unshakable purpose of direction and penetrating vision excel even wish-fulfilling gems, for they eradicate all the sufferings of samsara and the lower realms and bring quick attainment of high spiritual status and final realization.

Of these two, it is very useful to begin by cultivating the former, for faith makes one into a vessel suitable for receiving Dharma. To be more specific, one should cultivate the three types of faith; the faith of conviction, which understands the unfailing laws of karma and recognizes that positive and negative actions of body, speech and mind produce happiness and misery respectively; clear faith, that arises by perceiving the excellent qualities of a Guru, the Triple Gem, etc., and brings clarity to the mind; and wishful faith, that attempts to strive at progressing along the stages of the path to spiritual liberation.

These are the three general types of faith to be cultivated. The special faith of the tantric path is explained in *The Tantra of Excellent Accomplishments:*[2]

One should see one's tantric master
As being in fact a perfect Buddha.

A disciple with such wise respect
Holds attainment in his very hand.

All the Sutras and Tantras proclaim that cultivating a spiritual direction is the root of all religious experience. Therefore generate clear faith for your teacher and meditational deity and make firm the faith of conviction in the Dharma of the Secret Path. If this type of spiritual confidence is not maintained, not only during Dharma events but also throughout daily activities, one will not have the ability to clear away the mud of the mind and consequently will gain no grip on the basis of the path. Strive at the methods that imbue faith in the Dharma.

What are these methods? The principal one is mentioned in the chapter on faith of the text *Selected Sayings of the Buddha*:[3]

Do not rely upon the faithless
Who are like dry wells.
By digging in a dry well
We extract only a foul stench.
The wise rely upon the faithful,
Who are like vast lakes
Of waters clear, cool
And free of all mud.

The beginner should try to associate constantly with good friends in possession of both faith in and mindfulness of the Dharma, should listen to Mahayana master expound the holy Dharma, and should repeatedly contemplate the meaning of the teachings he has heard until he arrives at a definite understanding of them.

The scripture *Advice Given by Vajrapani, Lord of Secrets, to the Mahasiddha Karmavajra*,[4] states:

"O Karmavajra, to say one has seen the face of one's meditational deity and generated a sublime experience when one has not even attained faith in the Guru is to lie. To say one has renounced samsara when one has no faith in meditation upon impermanence and death is to lie. To say one does not create evil even though one has no real conviction in the karmic laws of cause and effect is to lie. To say that one's back is turned to samsaric pleasures although one has not meditated thoroughly upon the faults of samsaric indulgence is to lie. To say one has generated love, compassion and the bodhi-mind when one does not have an atom of concern for others is to lie. And to say one understands emptiness when one has not seen the untrue nature of all conventional things is to lie.

"O Karmavajra, if you have interest in the holy Dharma, approach it with faith.

"What are the causes engendering faith? Faith is aroused when one visualizes one's Guru as a second Buddha. Faith is aroused when one associates with spiritual people. Faith is aroused when one contemplates impermanence and death. Faith is aroused when one thinks of the laws of karma. Faith is aroused when one looks at the shortcomings of samsara. And if on the basis of these understandings we see the Guru as a boat by which we can free ourselves from samsara and subsequently we attempt to practice as he has instructed and not to degenerate our spiritual relationship with him, great benefits will accrue."

Especially, at the time of receiving tantric empowerments or initiations one should not see the Guru or meditational deity as being superior or inferior to one. Approach the various phases of initiation, such as requesting the empowerment three times and so forth, with a visualization of the two as being of one nature.

It is very important to appreciate these fundamental causes of a spiritually meaningful life. In this context the incomparable master Atisha wrote:

This body with freedom and endowments
So difficult to find, has been gained.
To find it again will be difficult.
Use it to practice Dharma
And thus make life meaningful.
Buddha has come, the Sangha are flourishing;
You have won a rare human form
And have met with the difficult-to-meet Guru.
Do not make it all for nothing.

We have achieved a precious human incarnation having the freedom and endowments necessary for Dharma practice, a form difficult to win and, once won, most meaningful. We have also met with the precious Sutra and Tantra doctrines of Buddha and with the spiritual friends and Gurus who are able to teach these to us.

Now that we have the opportunity to listen to Dharma, to contemplate its meaning and to meditate upon it, we should strive to take its essence.

Were life such that one could be assured of continually regaining a human form after death, perhaps there would be no need to make a great effort in practice now. One could work to attain liberation and the path to omniscience in a future life. But in actual fact the possibilities of regaining a human body in future lives indeed are slender. Now that we have met with the Dharma we should try to generate the light of wisdom able to cultivate goodness and to eradicate evil.

As for the practice of Dharma, remember the words of the great and omniscient Panchen Lama:

> When we point a searching finger
> Down our throats to analyze
> The nature of our previous ways,
> We see a fox wearing a lion's skin:
> We feign Dharma but don't really practice it.

When the mind is lost and overpowered by delusion, how can a spiritual thought even arise? Let alone a positive thought, even a neutral thought is rare. The body, speech and mind flow on in an unbroken stream of non-virtue and negativity. With motivation controlled by forceful delusion, even our attempts to practice Dharma usually end in collecting nothing but negative karma with the Guru. Evil is like a huge river cascading downhill, but progress is small and intermittent. Even when we strive intensely with strong conviction it requires much effort to pass beyond lower rebirth.

The master Nagarjuna said:

> From non-virtue comes suffering
> And all lower rebirths.
> From virtue comes high rebirth
> And happiness in all future lives.

When the karmic cause is negative, the karmic fruit is lower rebirth and misery. But when the karmic cause is creative, the karmic fruit is higher rebirth and happiness. This law is unfailing.

Perhaps you will think that rebirth in the lower realms is not so bad because, after that life-form has ended, you will again die and will then once more take a high rebirth. Remember the words of *A Guide to the Bodhisattva's Way of Life:*[5]

If one continues in negative ways,
A human rebirth will not be gained.
If a human rebirth is not found,
Only evil and never goodness follow.

If we do not generate virtue now
While we have the power to do so,
When later we are obscured by misery in the lower
realms,
What will we be able to do?

If now I create no goodness
But only collect more evil,
Then for a hundred million aeons
I will not hear even the sound of happy states.

In the lower realms one does not have the wisdom able to understand what to cultivate and what to avoid. Much evil is then collected and it becomes very difficult for even a thought of goodness to arise. Consequently, even when one's lifespan in a lower realm is over one just takes another lower rebirth and becomes lost for aeons in a vicious circle. How will the cause of high rebirth be then cultivated? Rather than let yourself go from light to endless circles of darkness, use this human life to go from light to light, from happiness to happiness.

You may think, "Fine, I will strive to accomplish the eternally beneficial; but later. First I should set straight the concerns of this life." Remember the chapter on impermanence in *Selected Sayings of the Buddha*:[6]

I did that, I am doing this,
And then will do that:
Thus men lay their plans.
But death strikes suddenly
With sickness and old age.

Plans may be made for the next hundred years, yet there is no certainty that any of them will be accomplished. However, this body degenerates and comes closer to death every year, month, day, hour and moment. Its lustre is fading, the power of its senses is fading and the mind is losing its clarity. These are but a stream of the sufferings of the ageing process. In the end we can expect death, like a man living in a jungle inhabited by lions, tigers, poisonous snakes and other such terrible, ferocious animals who are unable to live in harmony with one another and love to take life. If one finds oneself in such a jungle, where death could strike at any moment, it would not be wise to sit complacently.

Externally, all the various human and non-human harmful forces sit watching us, waiting for the fruit of our negative karma to ripen so that they can create interferences to our body, life, possessions, happiness and so forth. Internally, the four elements of the body—earth, air, fire and water—and the essential triad—wind, bile and phlegm—by nature hold the constant possibility of disease, and like wild animals of the jungle are continually fighting with one another for supremacy. When one gains power over the others, the suffering of disease and perhaps even death immediately fall upon us.

You may think, "But my body and mind are healthy at the present moment"; yet this also is not a valid reason for complacency.

The Omniscient Great Fifth (Dalai Lama) said:

> Black hair turns white as snow,
> A white face turns black as night,
> A body grown straight bends like a bow,
> Sensual objects give no pleasure.
> This is the pressure of old age.
> Wives and servants cannot help,
> The things of the past also are lost
> And friends and relatives just await their inheritance.
> This is the Messenger bearing
> An invitation from the Lord of Death.

Investigate the present condition of your body. The fact that it has never in the past ceased growing and evolving is an omen that it is held in the clutch of the agents who lead us to the other shore, the terrible land of the Lord of Death. Especially in this degenerate age when the human lifespan is so short it is rare to meet a man more than fifty or sixty years of age: and even were we to live this long ourselves, when we deduct the time spent in childhood, old age, sickness, sleep and so forth, not much is left for Dharma practice. Perhaps a year or two is given to serious practice. And most of one's life already has been spent on the meaningless.

To quote *Kanika's Letter*:[7]

> The Lord of Death comes suddenly
> To those who lack awareness.

Do not wait for tomorrow;
Practice the holy Dharma now.

Saying "I will do this tomorrow"
Is not the way of a wise man.
Have no doubt that death is sudden,
And that you will be reduced to nothing.

There is no certainty that the unpredictable hand of the merciless Lord of Death will not fall on us this year, this month, this day or even this very hour. The sun that will rise tomorrow morning may find our body in a charnel ground or on the funeral pyre surrounded by friends and relatives performing our death rites. Who can know this will not happen to him?

The great Tzong Khapa said:

What living being can say
He will not be swallowed by the demon of death?
When this is my sure fate,
O mind, how can you sit complacent?

Leave aside essenceless work
That anyway at death must be abandoned,
No matter how much energy one gave to it.
Think instead of how to progress along the path to
  enlightenment.

With this thought make firm
Spiritual qualities like humility,
Mindfulness, alertness and mental clarity.
Tame the difficult-to-tame mind.
Then at death the mind will rest in joy.

Whether one is a pandita who has mastered the five categories of knowledge, a mahasiddha who has occult powers, a king who rules with total control over many people, a warrior with strength and skill in fighting, or a farmer who lives his life under the weight of household life, in the end one will not escape death. From the very moment of birth all people enter into the path leading to death, regardless of whether they are high, medium or low. Nor is there any certainty when that death will come to them. For them to become distracted in worldly work is like a criminal condemned to death tomorrow wasting his time today on works which benefit this life alone. How ridiculous!

What benefits and what harms both this and future lives? The chapter on karma in *Selected Sayings of the Buddha*[8] says:

If you fear misery
And do not enjoy pain,
Then create no evil karma
Openly or in secret.

And also:

Evil is not like milk
That can suddenly change in nature.
It is like a hot coals covered in ashes that
Burn children who have long forgotten them.

Evil karma is not like a weapon
That perhaps will not cut us;
Carried forever into future lives,
Sooner or later it strikes.

Very intense evil karma produces the fruit of suffering within this very lifespan, and even if it does not ripen in this life it will not lose its potency even in a hundred countless aeons. The time shall come when it will manifest and bring suffering down upon us.

Alternatively, positive karma immediately brings a degree of happiness to the mind and in the future brings a happy rebirth conductive to further Dharma practice. Ask yourself, "What positive karma have I generated; what negative karma have I generated, what am I doing now and what do I plan to do in the future?"

The doors through which we collect both black and white karma are the body, speech and mind, Yet whether an action of body and speech is positive or negative depends solely upon the state of the mind. This was pointed out by the great master Aryadeva in *Removing the Veils of the Mind:*[9]

Placing two boots on the head of Buddha
Out of a positive motivation
And taking them off again
Both lead to rebirth as a king.
Therefore an action is meritorious or evil
Solely in dependence upon the state of the mind.

This refers to the famous story of a man who, on seeing water dripping onto the head of a Buddha image, placed his boots on its head to protect it. A second man who saw this thought it improper because boots are unclean, and so removed them. It is said that both men produced an equal amount of good karma, and both were reborn as kings. Thus it is most important to be clear on the nature of your motivation.

The significance of establishing the basis of a positive attitude towards all activities is stressed by the great spiritual master Geshe Potowa:

> All teachings in the *Kanjur* and *Tenjur*
> Are said to be methods for improving the mind.
> When the mind is unchanged then practices of body and speech
> Do not cause freedom, though one perseveres a hundred aeons.
> All practices of study, reflection and meditation
> Are but tools to refine the mind.

In brief, as the three *yanas* taught by Buddha, which includes all the teachings of the Hinayana and Mahayana Sutras and the four classes of Tantras, are in reality only methods and techniques for gaining control over the mind, we should use them solely for that purpose. One's every Dharmic activity—be it study, reflection, meditation or merely reading a scripture—should be used as a method for disciplining one's own mind. Then Dharma in theory and the reality of the practitioner's way of life will never contradict one another. This is extremely important. If we take this pragmatic approach ourselves then whatever we study is useful, every teaching is relevant, and we can see how every line of scripture is of immediate and far-reaching benefit to sentient beings.

Yet of all the high, medium and low teachings given by Buddha in accordance with the capacities, attitudes and karmic inclinations of the diversity of living beings, it is said to be most expedient to enter the Mahayana teaching from the very beginning.

The nature of the Mahayana is described by the great master Shaddhakaravarma:

> The Bodhisattvayana has two paths: the Paramitayana, or Transcendent wisdom Vehicle, and the Guhyamantrayana, the Result Vehicle of Secret Mantra.

Buddha set forth two principal Mahayana vehicles: the Paramitayana, the Vehicle (which provides meditation) on the causes (of enlightenment, or the Vehicle of signs; and the *Guhyamantrayana*, the Vajrayana, the Vehicle (which provides meditations) on the Results (of enlightenment). Yet practice of solely the former of these produces enlightenment only after three countless aeons of difficult austerities such as sacrificing limbs of one's body and so forth. In short, it is a long and arduous journey. But if in our practice we couple the Vajrayana with the Paramitayana then after a short comfortable practice we can go to the end of cultivating goodness and overcoming negativity and can quickly and easily gain the state of all-pervading Vajradhara within one lifetime.

Vajrayana is a very quick path; but in order to embark upon it we must first train our mindstream through the disciplines of the common path, the Paramitayana, until a degree of stability has been gained. Only then should one enter into the path of the Secret Mantra.

As *The Root Tantra of Glorious Chakrasamvara*[10] states:

> When the practices of the Sutras (are strong), the horizon of the secret yogas is (in sight).

Also the *Vajra Song*[11] says:

> The Kriya Tantra is for inferior men,
> Above this is the Charya Tantra;
> Then is the supreme Yoga Tantra for supreme beings
> And above this is the Anuttra Tantra.

The master who gives a tantric empowerment or initiation should explain to the disciple the exact nature and classification of the tantric system into which he is being introduced. He should also explain the distinguishing characteristics of the numerous lineages of transmission extant and relate a brief history of the lineage. He should elucidate the benefits and necessity of the transmission ceremony, the nature of the mandala being introduced, the function of the empowering Vajra-master, the characteristics required of the disciple receiving the empowerment, and the stages of the empowerment to be followed. These procedures can be understood either from the general tantric treatises or specific lineage manuals. If the master does not have time for such elaborate preliminaries he can reduce the above to a concise explanation of the specific qualities of the meditational deity in question.

One of the most important preliminary steps in the

empowerment and initiation ceremonies is the taking of the bodhi-mind pledge. This is because the practice of any Vajrayana system is a Mahayana Dharma only when the practitioner applying himself to it actually has the bodhi-mind. This was clearly pointed out by Lama Tzong Khapa:

> When practice of spiritual discipline
> Is not coupled with the bodhi-mind,
> It does not produce the bliss of Buddhahood.
> The wise therefore cultivate the supreme bodhi-mind.

And also:

> It is not enough to have a Mahayana Dharma. The practitioner himself must be a Mahayanist. Furthermore, the quality that makes one a Mahayanist is nothing other than the bodhi-mind: if one has the bodhi-mind one is a Mahayanist; if one doesn't have it one isn't on the Mahayana. Dedicate yourself to cultivating the bodhi-mind.

As said here, if we have the bodhi-mind we are Mahayanists and all our practices become Mahayana. If we use a so called Mahayana method without the basis of the bodhi-mind, then even if our renunciation is so great that we see all sensual pleasures in samsara as a terrible pit of fire, or we have meditated for a hundred aeons upon the ultimate nature of Being, the view vast as the sky, or have applied ourselves diligently to the profound tantric systems by means of receiving empowerments, transmissions and discourses and engaging in the powerful tantric yogas, our mind does not touch the Mahayana path.

As is said in *The Laying Out of Stalks Sutra*:[12]

> O son of noble family, the bodhi-mind is the very essence of the teachings of the Buddha.

If we wish to have a flower or fruit, we have to plant the corresponding seed. One cannot plant an apple seed and expect to get a marigold. The bodhi-mind is the seed giving birth to all Mahayana paths: it creates, maintains and fulfills the qualities of a Buddha.

The beneficial effects of the bodhi-mind are described in many Sutras, Tantras and Shastras.

The great Bodhisattva Shantideva wrote:

It is a supreme elixir
To destroy the Lord of Death,
An inexhaustible treasure to remove
The poverty of living beings.

It is a supremely powerful medicine
To pacify the diseases of beings,
A tree giving shade to pilgrims
Long wandering on the roads of life.

It is a ladder leading out
Of terrible states of suffering,
A moon shining in the mind
To disperse the pain of delusion.

It is a great sun to clear away
The ignorance clouding the minds of beings,
And the essence of butter produced
By churning the milk of Dharma.

If the disciple does not have this special mental quality, then, let alone giving him a tantric empowerment or initiation, he should not even be permitted to see a *mandala* or *mudra*. *The Tantra of the Vajrapani Empowerment*[13] states:

> O Manjushri, if any disciple has meditated upon and attained a measure of the bodhi-mind, that bodhisattva stands in the gateway of the Vajrayana because of his Bodhisattva ways. He should be given the empowerment of great wisdom and introduced into the mandala. A disciple without the qualification of the bodhi-mind should not be permitted to see the mandala. He should not even be shown *mudra* or *secret mantra*.

Therefore prior to receiving a tantric empowerment or initiation one should generate a pure motivation based on the bodhi-mind. This does not mean reciting certain verses, for how can words substitute for a state of mind? It means actually generating the bodhi-mind step by step, like a carpenter builds a house.

What exactly is the bodhi-mind? This is elucidated by the Venerable Maitreya:

The bodhi-mind is the wish for perfect bodhi
In order to accomplish the welfare of the world.

The thought which wishes to attain the state of perfect Buddhahood in order best to be able to benefit all other sentient beings is the phenomenon called the bodhi-mind.

In order to develop this state of consciousness one must cultivate two qualities: the thought which is concerned with other sentient beings and the thought which is concerned with enlightenment.

As for the first of these, the *Letter to a Disciple*[14] states:

> Animals eat plenty of grass when hungry
> And drink cherished water when thirsty;
> Why say they do it to benefit others?
> But there are supreme beings concerned
> Solely with the benefit of the world.
>
> Like the sun they illuminate the entire earth,
> Like the earth itself they support
> The burden of living beings.
> These great beings, free from personal interests,
> Strive to give the taste of happiness to others.

A horse's motivation is always simple: it seeks grass with which to chase away hunger and water with which to chase away thirst. In brief, it thinks only of its own needs. This is a quality common to most animals. But the quality of a supreme being's mind is that it has turned its back on self-interests and thinks only of ways to benefit others. Thus it is like a sun untiringly illuminating the lives of sentient beings dwelling on the four continents, and like the great earth which carries the weight of all that lives upon its surface. The Bodhisattva in possession of it no longer has any liking for self-centered works. He concerns himself solely with methods to produce benefits and happiness for the limitless sentient beings.

Why should we develop an altruistic attitude towards others? Because in all samsara there is not a single living being who does not want happiness and does not want to avoid even the smallest suffering. However, delusion and mental distortion have overpowered them and they are helplessly propelled into destroying their own happiness and well-being. Each of them is his own worst enemy. Forced by their own ignorance, attachment and aversion to collect a constant stream of negative karmas, with every action of their body, speech and mind they accumulate only further causes for rebirth in the lower realms of existence. As a result, many of them have taken rebirth in hell, where the great suffering of heat, cold and violent torture are experienced, pain one moment of which exceeds the total suffering of all humanity. Others have become hungry ghosts, who, although they search for a hundred years, rarely find even a dry gob of spit to eat or drink. Their sufferings of hunger, thirst, cold, heat and so forth are unimaginable. Still others have taken birth as animals and suffer terribly because of stupidity, domestication and so forth. Unable to generate a spiritual thought for even a moment, they have no chance of working for enlightenment.

Even those who have been reborn in the so-called higher realms must endure tremendous suffering. In the human realm there is the suffering of not getting what one wants, of having to nervously guard the things one has collected, of meeting with unpleasant people or circumstances, of being parted from loved ones and so forth.

The supreme sage Vasubandhu wrote:

All the sufferings of the lower realms
Manifest in the life of man.
He has the hell of intense pain,
The hungry ghost quality of destitution,
And the animal sufferings of being used and abused
By others of superior strength and cunning.
These sufferings flow constant as a river.

Some men are physically poor,
Others, though rich, are poor in contentment.
These intense sufferings of destitution
Attack and kill the two.

The mental and physical sufferings of man are his hell experiences, and his poverty and destitution are his experience as a hungry ghost. The man who is used by others of superior strength or intelligence, who is too poor to secure his food or shelter, or who although wealthy knows no contentment or satisfaction with his material state, or who fights with or is killed by other men, knows the nature of an animal's suffering.

Concerning the power and glory of rebirth as a god, Vasubandhu also wrote:

When delusion is present,
Negative karma continues to arise

And in the end comes a fall.
Are these heedless ones not objects of pity?
The patient, chronically ill,
Knows not his own condition.

The man who is overpowered by attachment, anger, pride, jealousy, and so forth has been struck down by the worst of enemies. Based on this loss he collects a steady stream of negative karmas and at the end his life falls into the lower realms like an arrow plunging down to earth. This is the nature of the death of a god of the sensuous realm.

Even during his life he experiences much misery. He has the physical suffering of continually warring with the antigods, the various mental frustrations inherent in celestial life, the sorrow of witnessing his vitality wane, and so forth.

The gods in the lower of the sensuous realms suffer terribly. As well as described above, they know anguish in their old age because of the signs of death that appear to them. They understand that soon they must leave their celestial palace, friends, lovers, and state of constant pleasure, and must descend once again into the lower realms of existence, where suffering completely embraces life.

The true nature of life in the heavens above the sensuous realms are described by the great master Vira:

Everything in these three realms
Burns in the flames of impermanence;
A fire blazing in a forest
Consumes flowers as well as trees.

The gods on the peak of samsara,
Whose minds are constantly distorted,
Become captured by the noose of death
Like an elephant tied by a chain.

Brahma, lord of the Brahma Heaven,
Who dwells in the bliss of meditation,
Becomes struck by impermanence
And falls like a river over a cliff.

A thousand gods and
A hundred Universal Emperors
Meet with the time of death
Like open butterlamps in a windstorm.

Even should one be reborn in the formless realms above the peak of existence, when the time of death falls one is led away like an elephant with a chain around its neck. Brahma himself, who experiences only the bliss of meditative absorption, evolves toward death from the very moment of his birth like a river flowing to the ocean. They all die, leaving nothing and taking nothing with them. Like a butterlamp in the face of a savage wind, the life of even a Universal Emperor, is suddenly extinguished. When the time comes his lustre bears the sign of death.

Exalted Nagarjuna stated:

After happiness comes misery,
After misery comes happiness.
This world of man constantly rotates
Between these two poles.

No matter what pleasure one gains in samsara, one day it will end and pain will take its place. This is the nature of the world.

The Elimination of Suffering[15] says:

In this life we suckle
Upon our mother's breast,
But in another we drink her blood
And eat flesh from her back.

Thus turning on the wheel of becoming,
We forget a hundred people
Who once did serve us well,
Who are the same hundred people
Whom we ourselves did once serve.

As the wheel of karma carries us through life upon life, a woman whose breast we once sucked becomes an animal that we eat, and a servant becomes a lord with great power over us.

Even in this life our relationships with people change drastically. A little flattery turns an enemy into a friend and a few heavy words make a friend an enemy. Relationships with friends and relatives are at best unstable.

The great master Chandragomin wrote:

In the beginning, sensual indulgence
And sweet poison are the same:
Both give pleasure when consumed.
In the end, sensual indulgence

turn an enemy into a friend, but the more kindness we show to our delusions, the more they harm us. They are like a terrible enemy always watching us from their own distance, waiting vigilantly for an opportunity to strike.

When this is our constant situation, how can we sit complacently? From *The Tantra Requested by Subahu:*[17]

> Overpowered by karma and delusion,
> They are masterless, protectorless, and insecure.
> Helplessly they go from life to life
> In accordance with their positive and negative karmas.

Although the self does not substantially exist to have any power we are overpowered by delusion and grasp at a self. This has dominated our stream of thought from beginningless time, leading us from life to life. Helplessly we have wandered throughout samsara, being born alone, dying alone and experiencing suffering alone. No one else can take our fate for us. No one can really protect us. Whether we stay or move is determined not by the strength of our determination but by our karma and delusion.

From *The Four Hundred Verses:*[18]

> Impermanence harms everything,
> And he harmed by it knows no joy.
> Therefore it is said that everything
> Impermanent is by nature suffering.

All realms and life-forms of samsara, evolving from moment to moment, are impermanent. Whatever is impermanent has the fault of continual disintegration. Anything having a fault has the potentiality to agitate an imperfect mind. All mental agitation is by nature frustration and suffering.

Thus all the infinite sentient beings of the three realms are naturally enmeshed in misery. Yet each of them has been a mother to me in countless previous lives, carrying me in her womb and caring for me more than for even herself. At that time they protected me from all harmful elements and did all they could to help me. In many previous lives as my mother every sentient being has sacrificed limbs of her body and even her very life for me. But now our memory of these lives is clouded by the impact of death, transmigration and rebirth. How should I relate to all these sentient beings, my all-kind mothers?

From *The Aspirational Prayer in Seventy Stanzas*:[19]

> When I see pleasure delighting others
> May I generate higher joy
> And remain meditating on joyfulness
> As if my only dear son were happy.
>
> Having shed anger and attachment,
> The causes of harming or favoring others,
> May I accomplish the tasks of all three worlds
> Like accomplishing one's work for one's son.

One should rejoice in the good fortune of the sentient beings who previously gained a pleasurable position or experience that one could have had for oneself. Look toward them with the glad love of a mother for her only child. Wish solely for their happiness. To regard some with attachment and others with aversion would be ignoble. Hope only that their wishes and needs be fulfilled, and exert yourself in the methods that eliminate their sufferings and improve their level of happiness.

From *A Guide to the Bodhisattva's Way of Life*:

> Whenever your eye sees a sentient being,
> Look upon him with integrity and love.
> Think, 'In dependence upon living beings
> Will I attain perfect Buddhahood!'

All good things that exist, from the ephemeral pleasures of this life to the ecstasy of perfect Buddhahood, arise purely in dependence upon the kindness of other sentient beings. Regard everyone you meet as a friend and relative. See all beings through eyes of joy, and leave no effort unmade in the quest to benefit them. Yet although the happiness and welfare of sentient beings are to be fulfilled, a person himself bound in the chains of worldly existence can forget about being able to do anything to help others.

The Bodhisattva Togme Zangpo wrote:

> What worldly god has power to protect us
> When he himself is shackled
> In the prison of cyclic existence?

The most powerful worldly god, being himself limited by the fetters of cyclic existence, has no ability to fully benefit other sentient beings. Nor do the Shravaka Arhants or Pratyekabuddhas, who

8. Op. cit., *Tshoms.*
9. Tib., *Sems-kyi-sgrib-sbyongs.*
10. Tib., *dPal-'khor-lo-sdom-pa'i-rtsa-rgyud.*
11. Tib., *Do-rje-gur.*
12. Tib., *sDong-po-bkod-pa'i-mdo.*
13. Tib., *Lag-na-rdo-rje-dbang-bskur-pa'i-rgyud.*
14. Tib., *sLob-springs.*
15. Tib., *Mya-ngan-bsal-ba.*
16. Tib., *gZhun-nu-ma-bdun-gyi-rtogs-par-rjod-pa.*
17. Tib., *dPung-bzang-gis-zhus-pa'i-rgyud.*
18. Tib., *Bzhis-brgya-pa.*
19. Tib., *sMon-lam-bdun-cu-ma.* An English translation of this text is also available from the LTWA under the title *Aryasura's Aspiration and a Meditation Upon Compassion.*

CHAPTER TWO

The Amitayus/Amitabha Traditions

Within a state of emptiness, in front of me, from a PAM arises a lotus and from an AH a moon mandala. A red HRIH is on top of these. Light radiates from it and acts to benefit sentient beings. Then it absorbs again and completely transforms into Protector Bhagavan Ayurjnana, whose form is red, with one face and two hands in the gesture of meditative equipoise holding a vase of immortality filled with nectar. His feet are in the vajra posture and he is adorned with the major and minor marks. He is wearing precious jewelry and silken raiment, and is by nature clear and transparent light. An OM is on his crown, an AH at the throat and HUM at the heart; from these light radiates, inviting the Protector Ayurjnana surrounded by all the Buddhas and Bodhisattvas from their natural abodes. JAH HUM BAM HOH

They become inseparable. Then light again radiates from the seed syllable at his heart, inviting the initiation deities. I request them, "Please confer initiation on him." They then confer the initiation from vases filled with water. The overflow at the crown of his head transforms into Amitayus as Nirmanakaya.

(The offerings are purified into emptiness)

OM SVABHAVA SHUDDHAH SARVA DHARMAH SVABHAVA SHUDDHO HAM

(To bless them, as in the highest yoga tantra)

OM A PARIMITA AYURJÑANA SAPARIVARA
ARGHAM PRATICHCHHAYE SVAHA
OM A PARIMITA AYURJÑANA SAPARIVARA
PADYAM PRATICHCHHAYE SVAHA
OM A PARIMITA AYURJÑANA SAPARIVARA
PUSHPE PRATICHCHHAYE SVAHA
OM A PARIMITA AYURJÑANA SAPARIVARA
DHUPE PRATICHCHHAYE SVAHA
OM A PARIMITA AYURJÑANA SAPARIVARA ALOKE
PRATICHCHHAYE SVAHA
OM A PARIMITA AYURJÑANA SAPARIVARA
GANDHE PRATICHCHHAYE SVAHA
OM A PARIMITA AYURJÑANA SAPARIVARA
NAIVEDYE PRATICHCHHAYE SVAHA
OM A PARIMITA AYURJÑANA SAPARIVARA
SHABDA PRATICHCHHAYE SVAHA

Within a state of emptiness, in front of me, from a PAṂ arises a lotus and from an ĀḤ a moon mandala. A red HRĪḤ is on top of these. Light radiates from it and acts to benefit sentient beings. Then it absorbs again and completely transforms into Protector Bhagavan Ayurjnana, whose form is red, with one face and two hands in the gesture of meditative equipoise holding a vase of immortality filled with nectar. His feet are in the Vajra posture and he is adorned with the major and minor marks. He is wearing precious jewelry and silken raiment, and is by nature clear and transparent light. An OṂ is on his crown, an ĀḤ at the throat and HŪṂ at the heart. From these light radiates, inviting the Protector Ayurjnana, surrounded by all the Buddhas and Bodhisattvas, from their natural abodes. JAḤ HŪṂ BAṂ HOḤ

They become inseparable. Then light again radiates from the seed syllable at his heart, inviting the initiation deities. I request them, "Please confer initiation on him." They then confer the initiation from vases filled with water. The overflow at the crown of his head transforms into Amitayus as Nirmanakaya.

(The offerings are purified into emptiness):

OṂ SVABHĀVA SHUDDHAḤ SARVA DHARMĀḤ
SVABHĀVA SHUDDHO 'HAṂ

(To bless them, as in the highest yoga tantra):

OṂ A PĀRIMITĀ ĀYURJÑĀNA SAPARIVĀRA
ARGHAṂ PRATĪCHCHHAYE SVĀHĀ
OṂ A PĀRIMITĀ ĀYURJÑĀNA SAPARIVĀRA
PĀDYAṂ PRATĪCHCHHAYE SVĀHĀ
OṂ A PĀRIMITĀ ĀYURJÑĀNA SAPARIVĀRA
PUṢHPE PRATĪCHCHHAYE SVĀHĀ
OṂ A PĀRIMITĀ ĀYURJÑĀNA SAPARIVĀRA
DHUPE PRATĪCHCHHAYE SVĀHĀ
OṂ A PĀRIMITĀ ĀYURJÑĀNA SAPARIVĀRA ĀLOKE
PRATĪCHCHHAYE SVĀHĀ
OṂ A PĀRIMITĀ ĀYURJÑĀNA SAPARIVĀRA
GANDHE PRATĪCHCHHAYE SVĀHĀ
OṂ A PĀRIMITĀ ĀYURJÑĀNA SAPARIVĀRA
NAIVIDYE PRATĪCHCHHAYE SVĀHĀ
OṂ A PĀRIMITĀ ĀYURJÑĀNA SAPARIVĀRA
SHABDA PRATĪCHCHHAYE SVĀHĀ

(The praise):

Amitayus, Protector and Bhagavan:
As you dispel the stains of sin,
I prostrate to your omniscient kaya
Which perceives all and so fills space.

(Request him strongly in prayer):

Emanating as many bodies as there are atoms,
To amitayus, The Protector, together with the Buddhas
  and their Sons, I prostrate
And make offerings, real and imagined,
Filling the whole of space.

I confess every sin and downfall
Accumulated since beginningless time.
I rejoice in the virtue of myself and others
And I implore all the Victors, never to depart to nirvana
But to turn the wheel of Dharma.
I dedicate this peerless virtue to supreme enlightenment.

Oh superb deity, Protector Amitayus,
Whose mere name destroys untimely death,
With your great untiring mercy
Listen to all beings and especially to one known as
  (oneself)
Confused and not realizing the great Dharmadhatu—
A state without coming or going
Because the nature of all dharma is free of signs since the
  beginning—
My mind thus corrupted, has accumulated black deeds,
  resulting in immense suffering.

Bless me by pacifying conditions
Leading to untimely death arising from
Humans or non-humans, and from
Degeneration of lifespan and merit by the power of
  previously accumulated sins.

Please confer the siddhi of immortality now
When I have brought together all that is good in samsara
  and nirvana,

Earth. With the altruistic thought that many people would benefit if they could recite the essence mantra of Amitabha, he explained the need for such a sadhana. In agreement, the custodial Bhikshu Lozang Kalzang Gyatso composed this brief sadhana in the temple Jinpa Jong at Gephelyong; it was dictated to the capable writer Namgyel Dorje.

Translated by Michael Richards, with Yeshe Lodro Rinpoche.

A Practice of Consciousness Transference involving Amitabha

(The Gateway to Sukhavati)

The Fifth Dalai Lama (1617–1682)

NAMO GURU MAÑJUSHRIYE

> I will unfold this method of transference
> To the blissful pure land—
> A tradition to use sleep skillfully as meditation—
> Described in the Prayer of Samantabhadra,
> Taken from the essence of the greater part
> Of the Last Turning.

Concerning this, it also says in the Prayer of Sāmantabhadra,
"When I am about to die..."

The following explains what is meant by the above lines which were uttered by great Mañjushri incarnate. It is a profound dharma, a guideline from the great mountain of lineages, passed down in a truly unbroken line.

There are four sections:

(1) preparation
(2) the actual practice
(3) the conclusion
(4) the benefits

(1) As the great Sakya translator Tsalmang Gyaltsen said:

> Go for refuge to the Three Jewels
> And then meditate on the bodhimind

faith, with the altruistic thought that many people would benefit if they could recite the essence mantra of Amitayus, he explained the need for such a sadhana. In agreement, the Buddhist Bhikshu Lozang Kalzang Gyatso composed this brief sadhana in the temple Jinpa Tong at Gartaryong. It was dictated to the capable writer Tsangkye Lodan.

Translated by Michael Richards, with Yeshe Lodro Rinpoche.

A Practice of Consciousness Transference involving Amitabha

(The Gateway to Sukhavati)

by

The Fifth Dalai Lama (1617-1682)

NAMO GURU MAÑJUSHRĪYE

I will unfold this method of transference
To the blissful pure land—
A tradition to use sleep skillfully as meditation—
Described in the Prayer of Samantabhadra,
Taken from the essence of the greater part
Of the Last Turning.[1]

Concerning this, it also says in the Prayer of Samantabhadra,
"When I am about to die...."

The following explains what is meant by the above lines which were conferred by great Manjushri on Acharya Jitari. It is a profound dharma, a guideline from the great mountain of lineages, passed down in a truly unbroken line.

There are four sections:

(1) preparation
(2) the actual practice
(3) the conclusion
(4) the benefits

(1) As the great Sakya translator Jamyang Gyaltsan said:

Go for refuge to the Three Jewels
And then meditate on the bodhi-mind.

Meditate on Amitabha before you.
And offer prostrations to him.

This means:

To purify sin through Amitabha Buddha, the yogin who wishes to be born in the pure realm of Sukhavati should clean his room and set up a painting with Sukhavati in the background, or if this is unavailable, place either a drawing or a model of Amitabha facing towards the east.

Set out whatever offerings have been prepared. Then lie on your right side on a comfortable bed, facing these. Just as you are about to drop off to sleep lying on your right side, turn your head to the west.

Visualize the Three Jewels transformed into Amitabha as the principal figure and his retinue. They are seated and pervade all of space. Then recite the four-line refuge formula three times, seven times or as many times as you like:

I take refuge in the Guru,
I take refuge in the Buddha,
I take refuge in the Dharma,
I take refuge in the Sangha.

Generate the bodhi-mind, thinking, "I will meditate on Amitabha in order to obtain Buddhahood to benefit all sentient beings." Imagine that your house and its surroundings are really the pure land of Sukhavati. Visualize yourself as the meditational deity.

On a precious throne before you with a lotus, sun and moon cushions, Amitabha is seated. He is red in color, with one face and two hands in the gesture of meditative equipoise holding an alms bowl full of nectar. His feet are in the Vajra posture. His garments are silk and he is adorned with the various ornaments of the Sambhogakaya.

He displays the 32 noble major marks and the 80 noble minor signs. In appearance the deity is void of natural existence, symbolized by a rainbow in the sky above. And he is pleased with you.

Imagine the root and lineage gurus, holy teachers of this dharma, are in a circle surrounding him. Behind them all the Buddhas and Bodhisattvas are seated, like banks of clouds.

While visualizing this, mentally offer the seven limb prayer three times, or the *Ten Preparatory Practices*, composed by Sakya

Pandit, or simply pay verbal homage by reciting the following lines composed by Pagpa Rinpoche:

NAMO BHAGAVATI AMITEBHYA

(Imagine you are offering flowers while reciting three times):

I take refuge in the Buddha Amitabha, who is the perfectly accompanied, completely pure Bhagavan, Tathagata and Arhat. I confess each and every sin and I rejoice in all merit. I implore all the Buddhas to turn the wheel of dharma and beg them to never depart to Nirvana. By this root of virtue may I acquire the state of Amitabha.

(2) The actual practice:

Generate confidence that one's sin has been purified.
Eliminate all craving.
And accomplish the single-pointed concentration of
 Amitabha
With a mind unafraid of death.

That is to say, generate a feeling of certainty that although your sin is a heap as high as Mt Meru, it has been exhausted by the force of the four powers:

(a) The power of relying on the circle of gurus, Buddhas and Bodhisattvas around Amitabha,
(b) The power of revulsion in the form of regret so great that the sins created up until now become purified,
(c) The power of preventing such actions in future by resolving never to do them again, even at the cost of your life,
(d) The power of applying all the antidotes in order to collect the necessary merit by offering the seven-limb prayer and so forth.

Eliminate all craving and attachment because when death comes, you must separate from the body of this life, from your wealth, relatives, close friends, servants and so on. Feel with confidence that after death you will go to Sukhavati, and without fear think about cyclic existence and the lower realms. Then three times sincerely pray:

Through Buddha Amitabha, the perfectly accomplished, completely pure Bhagavan, Tathagata and Arhat, I purify all my sins and obscurations. May he give me the prediction of my full enlightenment when I am born in the pure realm of Sukhavati.

When exhaling, your consciousness leaves in the form of white light from the left nostril. It enters the right nostril of Bhagavan Amitabha, moves through the channels within his kaya and dissolves into the HRĪḤ at his heart.

Then imagine that the mind of the Victorious Ones and your own mind have become one.

When this has taken your mind inside the seed syllable, from the heart of the Bhagavan white light in the nature of his mind comes from the HRĪḤ at his heart. It separates as would a flame taken from a butter lamp. This light leaves from his left nostril and enters your own right nostril, giving you well-being.

As it dissolves into your heart, imagine that the mind of the Victorious One and your own mind become one.

Continue this as long as possible as there is no recommended number, not deviating from the above instructions and without pauses, like a whirling torch flame.

(3) The conclusions:

The merit field gradually absorbs into the center and your body.
Generate yourself as Amitabha, the Embodiment of wisdom.
Dedicate your virtue to all sentient beings.
And then meditate on him again.

Thus at the end of the session, the Buddhas and Bodhisattvas dissolve into the root gurus and their lineages. The gurus dissolve into Buddha Amitabha and Amitabha dissolves into light, entering along with the breath, and thus dissolving into yourself.

As you also dissolve into light, your mind mixed with the Buddha and meditational deity, visualize the generation of Amitabha as in the previous meditation.

Recite the mantra, as many times as possible:

OM AMITĀBHA HRĪH SVĀHĀ

If you have the time, to conclude recite the Prayer of Samantabhadra or if not, recite the following:

May I be born in that happy pure land,
Noble mandala of the Victorious One,

From an exquisitely beautiful holy lotus.
And may I also obtain a prediction from King Amitabha himself.

In conclusion, seal it by dedicating the merit with the prayer:

I dedicate this merit
So that I and all sentient beings
Take birth by Transformation in Sukhavati
And be cared for completely by Amitabha the Protector.

OṂ VAJRA MUḤ

The merit field dissolves into you, and you feel that Amitabha Buddha has gone to Sukhavati.

With your forehead, throat and heart protected by the lights of OṂ, ĀH, and HŪṂ, go to sleep keeping the aspiration to be transferred to Sukhavati and faith in this strong wish, not allowing the mind to change to other thoughts.

In your daily activities imagine your dwelling is the pure realm of Sukhavati and always meditate on being one with Amitabha. When you go out, imagine you are going towards Amitabha Buddha seated before you.

(4) The benefits:

The benefits are that you will not be harmed by evil spirits.
You will not suffer when you die,
In the Bar-do you will be cared for by the Munis,
And in future you will achieve liberation.

This means that in this very lifetime, because of practicing this yoga, you will have no sickness, evil spirits or obstacles, your life will be long, and by the compassion of Amitabha you will be spared the misery of a painful death.

Because you will be free of fear in the Bar-do state having left this body behind as a snake discards its skin, when you are reborn from a lotus in Sukhavati, to the west, you will listen to the Dharma from Amitabha. Thus it is said in the Ratnakuta Sutra. And because of practicing this guideline you will certainly achieve liberation.

This guideline of the scholars of India and the Translators of Tibet is unmistaken.
It was passed down from the protector Sakya Pandit Jamyang.

As it is easy to practice, may its virtue
Lead all sentient beings to the Blissful Pure Field.

The colophon: This "Gateway to Sukhavati, a Practice of Sleep Meditation from the `Prayer of Samantabhadra'" was requested by Lozang Paljor of Lhasa. In order to benefit ardent beginners, it was conferred in person by the All-pervasive Lord from Zhalu, The Great Scholar Rinchen Sonam, and the great scholar and abbot Lochog Dorje. Through their kindness, based on the root poem of venerable Sakya Pandit, I have summarized the meaning of Sakya Pandit's own commentary as well as the scriptures of the Noble King of the Doctrine.

The Zahor monk, Jamyang Gaway Shen-nyen (the Fifth Dalai Lama) composed this on the sixth day of the fifth month of the Iron Bird Year (1981 Tib. Calendar). It was dictated to a leading exponent of ritual dance, Bhikshu Ngawang Gonchog.

This translation by Michael Richards and Achok Rinpoche.

Notes

1. The third of the major teachings which Buddha Shakyamuni gave at Vashali.

CHAPTER THREE

Avalokiteshvara, The Bodhisattva of Compassion

A MEDITATION UPON FOUR-ARMED AVALOKITESHVARA

by

The Second Dalai Lama (1475-1542)

(With the aspiration to perform the practice of meditation and mantric recitation in accordance with the tradition of Avalokiteshvara in his four-armed form, firstly take refuge, generate the altruistic mind of enlightenment and reflect on the four immeasurable attitudes:)

I take refuge in the Buddha, I take refuge in the Teachings and I take refuge in the Spiritual Community until I gain enlightenment. By the virtue I gather by practicing giving and the other perfections, may I attain Buddhahood in order to benefit all beings.

> May all beings be endowed with happiness;
> May all beings be free of suffering;
> May all beings never be separated from happiness;
> May all beings abide in equanimity undisturbed by the
> eight worldly attitudes or preconceptions.

(Recite the above verses three times. Then confirm the emptiness of all phenomena in and beyond cyclic existence by means of the following mantra:)

> OṂ SVABHĀVA SHUDDHAḤ SARVA DHARMĀḤ
> SVABHĀVA SHUDDHO 'HAṂ

Everything becomes emptiness. Within the sphere of emptiness appears the letter PAṂ. It transforms into a white lotus upon which is the letter ĀḤ. ĀḤ becomes a moon disc; at its center is my own mind in the form of a white letter HRĪḤ. HRĪḤ emits rays, which work the weal of sentient beings, transferring them to the rank of a Superior. The rays re-collect into the letter HRĪḤ which transforms, and I emerge as the venerable Superior Avaloki-teshvara with a snow-white body, one face and four arms. The front pair are clasped together at my heart, the rear right one holds a crystal-jewel rosary of one hundred and eight beads, and the rear left one holds a lotus which blooms beside my ear.

I sit in full-lotus posture and am adorned with eight precious ornaments: for my head, ears, throat, hands and feet. I am clad in silken raiment and have an entrancing, serene smile. The letter OṂ marks the crown of my head, ĀḤ my throat, and HŪṂ my heart. Also, a white letter HRĪḤ sits at the center of a moon disc in my heart. HRĪḤ radiates lights, inviting the mighty Superior Avalokiteshvara and retinue of Buddhas and Bodhisattvas from their southern abode: JAḤ HŪṂ BAṂ HOḤ; they absorb into me and thus we become one.

Again light goes forth from the HRĪḤ at my heart, inviting the Empowering Deities.

I call to them, "Pray, grant me initiation."

Thus requested, they raise aloft vases full of wisdom nectar. (Intoning) OṂ SARVA TATHĀGATA ABHIṢHEKATA SAMAYA SHRĪYE ĀḤ HŪṂ; they initiate me with their nectars, which fill my body and purify all my defilements. The superfluity remaining upon the crown of my head as a protrusion transforms into the Buddha Amitabha, who becomes my crown ornament.

(Then make the offerings, which clear interferences, purify and invoke blessings:)

> OṂ ĀRYA LOKESHVARA SAPARIVĀRA ARGHAṂ (and so forth, until SHABDE) PRATĪCHCHHAYA SVĀHĀ.

White in color and untarnished by faults,
The Buddha Amitabha embellishing the crown of your head,
You gaze upon sentient beings with overwhelming compassion:
To Avalokiteshvara I humbly bow down.

(Then:)

Visualizing myself as Avalokiteshvara, at my heart appears a circular white moon-disc, upon which is my own mind in the form of a white letter HRĪḤ. At the periphery of the disc stand the six essence-syllables of the mantra OṂ MAṆI PADME HŪṂ. They are in block letters and are resplendently white like the rays of the rising moon.

Light comes forth from the syllables, filling my whole body and purifying all my negativities and obscurations. The rays then leave through my pores and purify the negativities and obscurations of all sentient beings, thereby conferring upon them the status of the mighty Superior Avalokiteshvara.

My three-fold manner of perception involves seeing all external appearances as rainbow-Deity forms of the mighty Superior Avalokiteshvara; all sound is heard as the six syllable mantra; and mind is imbued with the essence of method conjoined with wisdom, which is the great compassion focussed on all sentient beings and the wisdom understanding emptiness, or the wisdom which clearly perceives that all phenomena in and beyond cyclic existence lack even a particle of inherent existence and are but mere imputations.

Thus visualizing oneself as Avalokiteshvara melded within this three-fold ambit, one recites the Mani mantra. From the energy of the practice, all the sentient beings of the six realms obtain the Deity form of the Superior Avalokiteshvara. Moreover, in the manner of a full sesame pod, the entire earth, air and sky are filled with the form of Avalokiteshvara. Their combined chanting of OṂ MAṆI PADME HŪṂ releases the sound of the Mani mantra like a crescendo of thunder. Contemplating thus, recite OṂ MAṆI PADME HŪṂ as many times as possible.

Yet just OṂ, having the three-fold aggregate of A-O-M, signifies the three indivisible adamantines of my body, speech and mind. This mantra is called "The Jewel Holder," for a single enumeration with such perspicacity is meritorious. Thus OṂ starts the mantra.

Mani means jewel. Padma means lotus, whereas Padme denotes supplication. So with my heartfelt entreaty to Avalokiteshvara, who is "The Jewel in the Lotus," one recites the mantra while dwelling on contemplations such as of the fusion of the mighty Superior Avalokiteshvara's qualities within me.

Furthermore, the respective six syllables cut off the doorways to rebirth in the six realms of cyclic existence. The syllables are also the consummation of the six perfections. Thus the Mani mantra, having these and other excellent qualities, is held to be of endless advantage and significance. Moreover, the mighty Superior Avalokiteshvara is said to be in general the quintessence of all the Buddhas compassion and in particular the patron Bodhisattva of Tibet. Therefore one should strive with enthusiasm in the recitation, cultivating Avalokiteshvara as a most excellent Meditational Deity by dint of these special characteristics.

(To conclude the session:)

The entire visualized universe and its inhabitants, who are in the form of the Superior Avalokiteshvara, dissolve into me. I dissolve into HRĪḤ at my heart. HRĪḤ dissolves into the letter H. This vanishes like a rainbow in the sky.

(Contemplate thus with conviction.)

Then more within the sphere of emptiness I instantly arise in the form of the Superior Avalokiteshvara possessing the three-fold attitude described above, and at once engage in extensive deeds.

(End with peerless prayers and dedications of merit, such as:)

May I develop the peerless awakening mind which is latent within me; and may that which I have attained go from strength to strength.

May I enjoy repletion both spiritual and otherwise,
Never parted from my Perfect Master in all my lives.
By comprehensively amassing the qualities of the paths
and levels,
May I attain speedily the state of the Vajra Holder.

The colophon: This easily understood meditation upon the mighty Avalokiteshvara was composed by Gyalwa Gendun Gyatso at the insistence of several great Doctrine Holders.

Translated into English by Kevin Garratt with Chomdze Tashi Wangyal and Lozang Gyaltsen.

The Steps of Visualization for the Three Essential Moments[1]

(*A Stairway for Ascending to Tushita Buddha-field*) by

The Second Dalai Lama (1475-1542)

I prostrate to the Noble Avalokiteshvara.

I prostrate to you, the sole friend of all beings of the Three Realms. Having the banner of fame as Avalokiteshvara, you manifest the compassion and wisdom of countless Buddhas with skilful means to tame all beings.

Having fashioned here out of points from the sutras and tantras (beads of) practices for this life, death and the inbetween rebirth (or bar-do) period, I have strung this rosary of easily understandable words (condensing) Buddha's highest teachings.

The Noble Avalokiteshvara personally instructed the Indian

Master Practitioner Maitriyogi, the lord of the meditators. He in turn gave these teachings, known as "The Three Essential Moments" to (the Tibetan translator) Tro-pu Lotzawa Jam-papal. You should learn about the life of the venerable Maitriyogi, the pre-eminent qualities of this oral teaching and the practice of its preliminaries from the works of previous masters in which they are extensively given. Here I shall explain in easily understandable words the steps of the actual visualizations involved (in the practice of his teaching).

This is divided into two sections: (I) indicating the references for these (visualizations) in the root text and (II) how to practice the (specific) points of this.

I. *Indicating the References for these Visualizations in the Root Text*

> In this life meditate on your personal meditational deity.
> At the time of death meditate on the oral teachings of transference of consciousness.
> During the period in-between rebirths meditate on blending appearances.
> Continual meditation is important for all of these.

In this opening stanza from the root text the first line indicates the practice for this life, the second for the time of death and the third that for the in-between rebirth period. The fourth line applies to all of these. Thus, although transference of consciousness and the blending of appearances are imperative at the time of death and in-between period (respectively), you should practice them now in order to receive their desired benefit (at those times). As for how to do this, your practice should not be very intense one day and lax the next, but rather it should be steady like the flow of a river. This is important.

II. *How to Practice the Specific Points of This*

For this there are four sections: (a) how to do the practice of your personal meditational deity during this life; (b) an explanation of the practice of transference of consciousness at the time of death; (c) an explanation of the practice of blending appearances during the in-between rebirth period; and (d) a supplementary demonstration of the important points of philosophy, meditation and conduct.

IIA. How to Do the Practice of Your Personal Meditational Deity During This life

> Having remembered impermanence and suffering,
> Strongly generate great compassion.
> On the crown of your head (visualize) your Guru, in your heart the deity,
> Meditate on the non-independent arising of your own mind.

To practice the specific points of this, there are four sections: (1) oral teachings concerning the circumstances you must arrange (for success); (2) oral teachings concerning the actual Bodhicitta meditations: (3) oral teachings concerning the method of requesting your Guru and meditational deity; and (4) oral teachings concerning meditation on the non-independent arising nature of your own mind.

IIA1. Oral Teachings Concerning the Circumstances You Must Arrange for Successful Practice

This first point is indicated by the opening line of the second stanza of the root text. Thus when it says, "Having remembered impermanence" and "Having remembered suffering," the former means you should meditate on the impermanence of life, that is the fact that there is no certainty as to when you will die. This will cause you to turn away from your compulsive attachment to this life. The latter indicates the method for developing a genuine attitude of wishing Liberation from samsara. This is turning away from your compulsive attachment to the various so-called pleasures of samsara by recognizing the suffering nature of all the different realms of cyclic existence.

Taking these two as examples, you should at this point practice the various classes of meditation for training your mind on the stages of the Graded Path to Enlightenment when you are a man of (a) initial and (b) intermediate levels of motivation. These meditations are common, (that is prerequisite trainings for proceeding to the next stages). I fear, however, that if I were to outline these here this work would become too long. Therefore you should learn about these (meditations) from the "Lam-rim chen-mo" by the glorious Je Tzong Khapa.

IIA2. Oral Teachings Concerning the Actual Bodhicitta Meditations

This is indicated by the line, "Strongly generate great compassion." Without being interested only in liberating yourself from samsara, you must accept full responsibility for bringing about the happiness and benefit of all sentient beings by yourself alone. For this purpose you should train yourself to have a very strong desire to develop a supreme Enlightened Motive of Bodhicitta and follow the conduct of all Bodhisattvas.

There are two methods for training your mind to have such an Enlightened Motive. These are the seven-part cause and effect meditation and that of exchanging self with others. You should impress these on your mind from the "Lam-rim chen-mo" and the oral tradition teachings of the "Mahayana Training of the Mind."

IIA3 Oral Teachings Concerning the Method of Requesting your Guru and Meditational Deity

Until you become a Buddha by having developed a supreme Enlightened Motive and completing your two collections (of merit and insight), it will be impossible for you to liberate all sentient beings from samsara. Although this is so, it is imperative that all sentient beings receive protection and refuge right now from the unbearable sufferings of samsara (in general) and the three unfortunate rebirth states (in particular). (Realizing this and seeing that) you do not have the ability (to liberate them) now, think how necessary it is to request the Noble Avalokiteshvara and the thousand Buddhas (of this eon to be able to benefit them now).

(Visualize) on the crown of your head a flawless stupa of white crystal moonstone with a thousand doors,[2] transparent and having the nature of light. Within its vase-like sanctum on a mandala seat of a lotus and moon-disc (sits) your root guru in the form of the venerable Noble Avalokiteshvara. His body, white as a snow mountain, has one head and four arms. His first two hands are pressed together at his heart, the lower right hand holds a jewelled rosary of crystal and the lower left a white lotus flower. He sits with his feet crossed in the vajra posture, wearing precious jewelled ornaments and clothes of multicolored scarves, his heavenly body fully adorned with all the major and minor marks of a Buddha. Thus he appears in the midst of a great burst of rays, like a rainbow in the sky with no true independent existence. This is what you should envision first.

Then at each of the thousand doors (of this stupa) imagine the thousand Buddhas of this fortunate eon. All those on the east (at the front of your head) are white, in the form of Vairochana) those on the south yellow, in the form of Ratnasambhava; those on the west red, in the form of Amitabha; and those on the north are green, in the form of Amoghasiddhi. This is the way to visualize your guru on the crown of your head. Although several texts say to picture Avalokiteshvara in his Khasarpani form,[3] there is no difference in what this signifies. Nowadays more people who use (Avalokiteshvara's) six-syllable mantra recite it while visualizing his four-armed aspect. Therefore I have arranged (these practices) accordingly.

As for how to see the deity in your heart, (this is as follows). Visualize at your heart a red, thousand-petalled lotus, slightly opened with the petals standing erect. At its center on a mandala seat of a moon-disc is (Avalokiteshvara) the meditational deity of great compassion, inseparable from your own mind and envisioned the same as on the crown of your head. On each of the thousand petals imagine a flawless white Ah, having the nature of light and glittering white. At Avalokiteshvara's heart there is a moon-disc with a white syllable HRĪḤ. Around its edge revolve the letters of the six-syllable mantra (OṂ MA ṆI PAD ME HŪṂ) like pearls strung on a rosary. Visualize this well.

Your faith in the Avalokiteshvara and thousand Buddhas of this fortunate era, visualized on the crown of your head, is so intense that tears stream from your eyes and the hairs of every pore of your body quiver. Your mind single-pointedly yearning and filled with great faith, (you should request as follows:)

"O great compassionate Guru-meditational deity. My mothers and fathers, all the beings of the six rebirth states, are drowning in the great ocean of samsara's suffering. They have no one to protect them, no refuge, these poor beings who are in such agony. I beseech you, please save them right now from this great ocean of samsara's suffering. I implore you, please free them this instant. I beg you to liberate them on this very spot!" This is how you should make your request, with intense yearning.

Then rays of light are emitted from Avalokiteshvara's body on the crown of your head and touch the Avalokiteshvara in your heart. And rays of light stream forth from the thousand Buddhas of this fortunate aeon and strike the thousand Ah's in your heart. From these thousand Ah's and the Avalokiteshvara in your heart streams of white nectar flow in immeasurable waves. The nature (of this nectar) is the wisdom of non-duality; it merely appears in this (white) form. This (nectar) now totally fills your body and all the obstacles and unripened consequences of your previous non-virtuous actions of body, speech and mind, together with their instincts, are purged. They completely leave you, oozing out blackly from every orifice and pore of your body in the form of tar, filth and scorpions. Your body becomes fully transformed into Avalokiteshvara, transparent and clear as polished crystal, radiant with the major and minor marks of a Buddha.

Streams of nectar now flow from all the pores and openings of your body. First they go down to the hell realms, completely filling every state of hell, purging all hell creatures of their sufferings of heat and cold as well as of the causes for these: their karma and delusions, (eliminating them) completely from their roots. They are fully purified. Then all their surroundings—the red-hot iron ground, the iron houses blazing with flames, the icy confines, the black darkness—all these unbearable things, their entire environment, instantly disappear. Everything totally transforms into a pure-land paradise, like the Sukhavati Buddha-field, precious by nature, broad, expansive, wide-open, soft to the touch and blissful. And all the beings living there become totally transformed, assuming the appearance of the heavenly body of the Noble Avalokiteshvara, having no true independent nature just like rainbows in the sky. This is what you should envision.[4]

Then streams of nectar flow forth in turn to every state of existence, to the hungry ghosts, animals, anti-gods, humans and to the gods of the Desire, Form and Formless Realms. They purge them completely of all their suffering, together with its causes: their karma and delusions. The hungry ghosts are freed of hunger and thirst; the animals of their stupidity, dumbness and devouring of each other; the anti-gods of their fighting and quarrels. No longer suffer do men from birth, sickness and death; the Desire Realm gods from death, transference and falling to lower rebirths; the gods of the Form and Formless Realms from the suffering of extensiveness. They are fully purified and all the lands they inhabit are totally transformed into pureland paradises like Sukhavati Buddha-field. And all the beings living there become totally transformed, assuming the heavenly body of the Noble Avalokiteshvara. This is what you should envision.

At this point if you wish to recite the six-syllable mantra (OṂ

MAṆI PAD ME HŪṂ, you should do so as follows). Visualizing yourself as the Noble Avalokiteshvara, imagine that as the sound of this mantra comes forth from your mouth it is likewise proclaimed from the mouths of all the beings you have transformed into Avalokiteshvara. It is as if the sound of this mantra causes the entire universe to shake. (In this way) recite it as many times as possible.

At the conclusion of your meditation session, visualize rays of light being emitted from the HRĪḤ in the heart of the deity within your heart, spreading out and striking all the lands you have been visualizing as Sukhavati Buddha-field. These places completely melt into light and dissolve into the beings inhabiting them, whom you have been envisioning as Avalokiteshvara. These beings then completely melt into light and dissolve into yourself. The Avalokiteshvara at the crown of your head melts into light and dissolves into the Avalokiteshvara in your heart. The thousand Buddhas of this fortunate aeon dissolve into the thousand Ah's in your heart. The stūpa vanishes like a rainbow in the sky. Then you yourself, whom you have been visualizing as Avalokiteshvara, dissolve into the lotus in your heart with the Ah's on its petals. This dissolves into the Avalokiteshvara at its center and he into the (moon-disc) seat in his heart, with the rosary of the six-syllable mantra around it. This then dissolves into the HRĪḤ at its center and finally even disappears into a state of clear mind without any object. Concentrate single-mindedly on such a state.

IIA4. Oral Teachings Concerning Meditation on the Non-Independent Arising Nature of Your Own Mind

This is divided into how to gain experience in the Identitylessness of the conventional "I" and in the Identitylessness of all phenomenal things. If I were to explain these in brief, (it would be as follows).

First of all, each of us has a very strong thought of an "I" that arises automatically in our mind-stream. If you examine this thought and how (this "I") appears, you do not see it as a mere appearance, as only the name "I" labelled onto your five aggregates. Rather, as the object of this thought, an "I" comes to mind that seems to exist truly independently as some "thing" on top of the five aggregates as if it were there from the beginning.

(Likewise) when you see something having the ability to function as a support, the thought "this is a pillar" automatically arises. When you examine this thought and this "pillar" appears, you do not see it merely as the name "pillar" labelled by your thought onto this piece of wood. Rather, on top of this object, which is just a piece of wood, there seems to appear something existing truly independently as a pillar. But although these things seem to exist truly independently in this way, there has never been any such thing as an "I" existing truly independently on top of an object, the five aggregates.

For example, other than (the mere name) "pillar" labelled by a conceptual thought onto a piece of wood functioning as a support, there has never been any such thing as a truly independent "pillar" existing on top of that object, a piece of wood. Yet there arises in all of us the thought that this is really a pillar, not just the name "pillar" used as a convention for this (piece of wood). However, you do not see that the name "pillar" is being used as a convention. This thing does not exist truly independently as a pillar; only subsequently has the name "pillar" been labelled onto it. Yet because there are conventions—such as saying, "I see the pillar" when you have seen this object—you grasp at it (as if it were a true "pillar"). But, not only is a pillar (merely) something labelled onto a piece of wood, there has never been anything whatsoever that has existed objectively as a truly independent pillar, even to the slightest extent.

Likewise, as soon as an infant is born, someone gives him a name, like "Tashi". Then whenever you see him, you think, "This is Tashi." But in this case also, even though it strikes you that this infant exists objectively as Tashi from his own stance, he does not exist objectively as a truly independent Tashi at all. This is because if he were to exist in this way, then even before he was given such a name, if you saw him it would only be possible to think, "This is Tashi." No other thought could arise. Therefore this infant exists as the so called "Tashi" merely by virtue of having been labelled thus by a thought.

By analyzing such examples, try to become firmly and thoroughly convinced that everything—your conventional "I", your aggregates and so forth—exist merely as mental labels that have been labelled by a conceptual thought onto their respective (and appropriate) objects of labelling. None of them exist as true, independent things on top of these objects, even to the slightest extent.

In meditation you should concentrate single-mindedly on such a conviction. During post-meditational periods, train yourself to see every appearance of an object that arises as (just) an appearance.

(Realize that) like an appearance these arise as if they were illusions, void of any objective existence established from their own individual substance.

I have explained here only briefly and simply how to gain experience in this view of Voidness. Please learn further about it from other texts in which this view is more elaborately presented.

IIB. An Explanation of the Practice of Transference of Consciousness at the Time of Death

The essence of the oral teachings concerning the time of death is how to practice transference of consciousness. This is indicated in the root text:

> Having made an offering of your body and given it away,
> Completely abandon all you rely on.
> Making use of a shaft of light,
> Hurl your mind into Tushita Buddha-field.[5]

The practice of this point is divided into three sections: (1) eliminating unfavorable circumstances for accomplishing transference of consciousness; (2) gathering the favorable circumstances and (3) the actual visualization for transference of consciousness.

IIB1. Eliminating Unfavorable Circumstances for Accomplishing Transference of Consciousness

If you are attached to and have compulsive attraction for places, your body or possessions, it is like a bird trying to fly in the sky with stones tied to its wings. No matter how much you wish to transfer your consciousness to Tushita Buddha-field, this transference will be prevented. To counteract this, you must block such attachment and compulsive attraction for your body. Therefore first you must offer your illusory body to the assembled Field of Merit, as indicated by the first line of this stanza.

To visualize clearly the Field of Merit, envision before you in space a broad and expansive jewelled throne supported by eight lions. Seated upon it on cushions of a lotus and moon-disc is your kind root Guru, seen as before in the form of the venerable Avalokiteshvara. Above his head are the Gurus of his lineage. Level with the upper part of this body are the meditational deities of the four tantric classes together with the assembly of deities from each of their mandalas, as well as all the Buddhas and Bodhisattvas.

Level with the lower part of his body all the Shravakas, Pratyeka-buddhas, Dakinis, Dharmapalas and Protectors are gathered together like billowing clouds. In addition, spreading out from the lower corners of the throne are all the invoked harmful spirits which bring you misfortune from the harm you have caused them in the past. Seated directly beneath the throne, without any space between them, are all the sentient beings of the six states of rebirth, headed by your kind mother and father of this life. This is what you should envision. In short, you should picture the entire earth, the heavens and all the space between completely filled as if by sesame seeds with all these invoked beings.

Then, as for how to accumulate merit, (this is as follows). You should think, "In samsara I have taken countless bodies of sentient beings in general and specifically I have taken countless human bodies. Yet every one of them has been meaningless. I have done nothing but waste them all. Not even once have I taken advantage of their essence and made them meaningful. Now in this life I have taken this awkward body and until now I have been unable to accomplish any pure Dharma practice that would be of benefit. Rather, to support this body, I have done so many kinds of non-virtuous actions.

"Now, as the time of my death (is approaching), I shall have to leave this body behind like the wild, barren pastures at the top of a mountain. Then the non-virtuous karma I have accumulated because of this body will bring me the unbearable suffering of a lower rebirth in my next life. Therefore, as it is so improper to be attached to this body, let me instead use it to complete in great waves and with ease my collection of merit. For this I must request help from my compassionate meditational deity."

At your heart visualize your mind in the form of the body of Avalokiteshvara, the size of a finger. All of a sudden he bursts forth from your heart and stands in the space before you—white, healthy, handsome, beautiful, glistening—looking back at your old set of aggregates,

Then request your Guru in the form of Avalokiteshvara before you, "O compassionate Guru-meditational deity, I beseech you to help me use my body to complete in great waves and with ease my collection of merit."

Having been requested in this way, Avalokiteshvara proclaims, "OṂ ĀH HŪṂ" and three human heads the size of Mount Meru appear forming a tripod. Then from the heart of the meditational deity a Dakini comes forth, holding a butchers' cleaver. Using this curved blade, she chops off the crown of the skull of your old body from its forehead up and lifts it off. It grows larger than a thousand, a million, a billion world systems and she places it covered with blood on top of the (human-head) tripod. This is what you should see.

Then once again many Dakinis come forth holding butchers' cleavers. They hack the flesh, blood and bones of your old body into little pieces and pour them into the skull-cup. It becomes filled to the brim with a great heap of flesh and blood.

Once more from the mouth of the meditational deity "OṂ ĀH HŪṂ" is proclaimed. All your flesh and blood is thereby transformed into the nectar of uncontaminated wisdom-knowledge, orange like the color of the sunrise. Even its aroma and texture brings blissful satisfaction to the minds of the Buddhas and Bodhisattvas and it is able to eliminate the sufferings of the six rebirth states. This is what you should envision.

Then many Dakinis come forth from Avalokiteshvara's heart, holding butchers' cleavers and skull-cups. They fill all of space. Using these skull-cups in their hands, they spoon out the nectar as if it were inexhaustible. Offering it to your root and lineage Gurus, to the meditational deities, Buddhas and Bodhisattvas, to the Shravakas, Pratyekabuddhas, Dakinis and Dharmapalas, they bring great blissful satisfaction and pleasure to all their minds. (In this way) envision completing your collection of merit in great waves and with ease.

In a similar fashion, (the Dakinis) give (nectar) to the invoked harmful spirits which bring you misfortune from the harm you have caused them in the past. Your karmic debt to them is thus cleared, their grudges are soothed and they are all transformed into Avalokiteshvara.

(The Dakinis) then present (nectar) to all the sentient beings of the six states of rebirth, headed by your kind mother and father. They are purged completely of all the suffering of their individual states, together with its causes: their karma and delusions. They are fully purified and, as before, all the lands they inhabit are totally transformed into pure-land paradises like Sukhavati Buddha-field. And all the beings living there become totally transformed into Avalokiteshvara. This is what you should envision. Then recite as before the six-syllable mantra.

At the conclusion of this, visualize all the lands melting into light and dissolving into the beings inhabiting them. These in turn dissolve into your mind (in the form of Avalokiteshvara, your Guru). Then the entire assemblage, from the lineage Gurus to the Dakinis and Dharmapalas (dissolve) into your root guru who is seated in space before you (in the form of Avalokiteshvara). He (the Avalokiteshvara) in turn dissolves into your mind, as a way of bestowing upon you waves of inspiring strength. Finally your mind itself disappears into a clear state without any object. This is what you should envision.

Thinking of how all (three) aspects of offering—the person who makes it, the offerings themselves and those to whom they are presented—are totally Void, not having even a speck of inherent independent existence, expand your wisdom and understand that these three spheres are not true objects existing unto themselves.

By practicing in this way, you will remove your attachment and compulsive attraction to your body. If, however, it happens that you are still not rid of your attachment and compulsive attraction to your friends, relatives, wealth and possessions, the way to block this is indicated by the second line of this stanza. No matter how many friends and relatives you may have in this life, it is due to the forces of previous karma that they have gathered together for but a brief moment like leaves blown together by the wind. In the end they will desert you and you will forsake them, for at the time of death not even a single relative or close friend will accompany you. You must go into the future completely alone. Thinking in this way, try to become unattached to them.

When you die your wealth and possessions are also left behind. Realize that you must travel on all by yourself like a hair pulled out of a lump of butter. Therefore, without any compulsive attraction and with no attachment give them away to virtuous causes, as offerings to the Three Jewels of Refuge and for the service of the monastic community. Do not have even the slightest attachment or compulsive attraction.

IIB2. Gathering the Favorable Circumstances for Accomplishing Transference of Consciousness

Set a very strong intention to be born in Tushita Buddha-field and offer many prayers to take such a birth. Dedicate all your roots of virtue as the causes for (transferring your consciousness) there.

IIB3. The Actual Visualization for Transference of Consciousness

This is indicated by the last two lines of this stanza. Visualize in the center of an encircling rosary of precious jewelled mansions called "The Dharma Palaces of Joyful Tushita", the precious jewelled palace of perfection in which resides the venerable Maitreya Buddha. It is called "The Palace of the Exalted Dharma" and "The Palace of the Lofty Banners". Before it is the courtyard in which the venerable Maitreya teaches the Dharma. It is of the nature of all precious gems, exquisitely delightful, broad and expansive, called "The Holder of the Dharma Bringing Joy to the Mind". In its center on a lion throne, called "The Excellent Dharma", sits the Buddha Maitreya, his golden body radiant with the light of a hundred thousand suns, resplendent and shining like Mount Meru. He sits facing Jambudvipa, our own Southern Continent, giving copious teachings to a circle of countless Bodhisattvas on the ways and methods of Prajnaparamita, the Perfection of Wisdom. With single-pointed yearning you must strongly wish to be able to witness (this scene) and receive these teachings yourself.

"O great compassionate Maitreya Buddha, please give me refuge from the fears of samsara and the unfortunate lower states of rebirth. I beseech you, please lead me right now to your Tushita Buddha-field of Joy. I implore you, please lead me there this instant. I beg you to take me on this very spot."

Having been requested in this way, the venerable Maitreya emits from his heart a long and straight shaft of light like an extended sleeve. It penetrates the aperture at the crown of your head, opening it up like a skylight. Then all at once, in the region of your heart, your mind takes the form of the divine body of Avalokiteshvara, the size of a finger. Looking up through the pathway of this shaft of light through the aperture at the crown of your head which has opened up like a skylight, you see directly the golden mandala at the heart of the venerable Maitreya, dazzling yellow as if polished and struck by the rays of the sun. With the triple awareness that the shaft of light is a pathway, that you must travel this path and must transfer your consciousness into the heart of Maitreya, request as before with intense yearning.

Then from the heart of the venerable Maitreya another light is beamed down inside this light-shaft, long and straight, in the form of a hook. It enters through the aperture at the crown of your head and, striking your mind which you have been visualizing in the form of Avalokiteshvara, it lifts it upwards all at once as if caught by this hook. Bursting forth from the aperture, it flies without any obstruction like a shooting star up the course of this light shaft and dissolves with relief into the heart of the venerable Maitreya. Feel that your mind and that of Maitreya have become fully mixed and are now of one taste. Remain for a while absorbed in this state.

Then once more you emerge from Maitreya's heart. Transmuted into a heavenly child with great intelligence and common sense, (you appear) in the center of a thousand-petalled lotus in the Dharma courtyard of the venerable Maitreya Buddha. Having taken this birth as someone with the good fortune to make abundant use of the Mahayana teachings, you drink insatiably the nectar of Maitreya's words.[6]

IIC. An Explanation of the Practice of Blending Appearances During the In-between Rebirth Period

The essential practice for the in-between rebirth (or bar-do) period is blending appearances. From the root text:

> Having understood this as the in-between state,
> Make the outer, inner and secret transformations.
> With the union of Voidness and compassion,
> The wise make connection with their next rebirth.

The first line of this stanza indicates the method for identifying the in-between rebirth period as such. As for how to do this, you should start right now to see every object that appears to you as a deceptive appearance of the in-between state. Meditate on this repeatedly, thinking how imperative it is to recognize the in-between period as such. Then when you are actually born in this state, you will be able to think, "Now I am born in the in-between state; all things that appear here are the appearance of the in-between state." In this way you will recognize this state as such, just as in a dream you can tell that what you are dreaming is a continuity of remembrances of the day.

The second line indicates the actual practices for the in-between rebirth period. The external transformation is as follows. From now on, whenever anything of the external physical world appears, seeming to have the inherent true nature of earth, a rock, a tree and so forth, meditate by thinking that these are the deceptive appearances that come from your being in the in-between state. They do not have any inherent true independent existence as such. Do not let your mind follow after these impure objects (grasping them as real). Rather, visualize these surroundings as totally transformed into a pure land paradise like Sukhavati Buddha-field.

The inner transformation is exactly the same. Whenever any beings appear—humans, animals or whatever—inhabiting these places, envision them all transformed into the divine body of the Noble Avalokiteshvara.

The secret transformation is as follows. Whenever any beings or their surroundings appear like this, seeming to exist objectively from their own stance, remember that all these appearances seem to exist in this way due only to the power of your own mind being corrupted with the instincts of grasping for true independent, existence. Meditate on how they do not have even a speck of objective existence established from their own individual stance.

Having meditated in this way, when you are born in the in-between state you will be able to transform whatever impure places appear, such as hells and the world of the Lord of Death, into a pure-land paradise like Sukhavati Buddha-field. Whatever beings appear there, such as torturers of hell wielding swords and chasing you, You will be able to change them all into the form of Avalokiteshvara. And anything whatsoever that appears, you will be able to transform into a state of Voidness without any inherent true independent existence.

The last two lines indicate how to take rebirth wilfully in samsara. This method for being reborn with a perfect (human) body fully possessing the complete liberties and endowments for the practice of Dharma is as follows. When you are in the in-between rebirth state and you see your future father and mother lying in union, an attitude of repulsion towards your father and attraction for your mother will arise if you are under the sway of being born as a male. When this happens, think about such things as how your father, the object giving rise to your repulsion and anger, has been kind to you from beginningless time. Turn back your aversion by meditating on strong compassion towards him.

(Likewise) meditating on how your mother, the object of your attraction and desire, is void of existing objectively and truly independently from her own individual stance, although she appears to exist in this way, turn back your attraction. Then take this rebirth letting yourself be thrown by the thoughts. "It is to be able to practice the rest of the path that I now take rebirth in this mother's womb. May I be able to fulfil in great abundance the purposes of sentient beings."

IID. A Supplementary Demonstration of Important Points of Philosophy, Meditation and Conduct

The essential point of philosophy is to recognize whatever
arises.
The essential point of meditation is not to be distracted
from this.
The essential point of conduct is to remember (that
everything has) an equal taste.
These are the teachings of the great Master Practitioner.

Thus whatever arises, although appearing to exist objectively from its own stance, you must recognize (its nature correctly). Being convinced that it does not exist in the way it appears is the essential point of philosophy. Meditating single pointedly without distraction on this point of which you have become convinced is the essential point of meditation. Training yourself with the Enlightened Conduct of the Bodhisattvas to work for the sake of others while in the state of remembering that everything of samsara and Liberation has the equal taste of Voidness as its nature is the essential point of conduct. This is the meaning of what the great Master Practitioner has taught.

The last line (of this stanza) indicates that everything previously explained was the teachings of the venerable Maitriyogi, thereby implying that this final stanza is not the venerable Maitriyogi's words. This concludes the explanation of the steps of practice for the work known as "The Three Essential Moments", which (has been composed) for easy comprehension and convenient practice.

These pearls of a profound path have come
From the ocean heart of the Holder of the Lotus
And have been strung on a thread to form the necklace
of this composition.
May it adorn the necks of those glorious ones of good
fortune.
By the virtuous white merit of my efforts here,
May all beings be freed from the abyss of unfortunate
rebirths.
In the immeasurable joyful delight of the fabulous Tushita
Buddha-field,
May they make abundant use of the nectar of the
Mahayana teachings.

These easily understandable words explaining "The Three Essential

Moments" have been composed by the most reverend expounder of the Dharma, (His Holiness the Second Dalai Lama), the glorious Ge-dun gya-tso, at the Tag-tzer Palace in Wol-ka, Tibet. They have been written to enhance the profound meditational practices of Ye-she cho-dron. This glorious and great benefactress of so many people extends her generous hand afar, giving the breath of life to the poor and needy. She has supreme and unshatterable faith in the teachings and those who uphold them. The scribe for this work was Sang-gyay gon-po.

Prepared at the Translation Bureau of the LTWA by Sharpa Tulku, Khamlung Tulku, Alexander Berzin and Jonathan Landow.

Notes

1. This work, for the most part, may be classified in the category of kriya tantra. Included in it, however, are certain practices of the anuttarayoga tantra, such as those concerning the in-between rebirth period (b'ar-do). Thus it is a mixed work composed by Maitriyogi for the specific needs of his disciples. For its practice only the kriya tantra initiation for Avalokiteshvara is required, and not necessarily the anuttarayoga one. A Heruka (Cakrasamvara) initiation empowers you to do any Avalokiteshvara practice.
2. The thousand doors may be visualized all in a row on one level around the stūpa, or stacked in level on each side, whichever way is more convenient.
3. The Khasarpani form of Avalokiteshvara is white, with one head and two arms. He sits in the half-vajra posture with his left leg crossed on his right thigh and his right leg bent and extended forward, resting on a lotus cushion. His right hand is in the gesture of giving protection, resting on his right knee with the palm facing outwards. His left hand is at his heart, holding the stem of a lotus which extends upwards above his left shoulder.
4. Sukhavati Buddha-field is presided over by Amitabha, the Buddha of infinite light and life. Thus Buddha is the Guru of Avalokiteshvara and has appointed him to make conditions conducive for Dharma study, to teach the Dharma and to lead all beings to the Buddha-fields. It is for this reason that Sukhavati is visualized in these purification practices.
5. Tushita Buddha-field is presided over by Maitreya, the fifth and next Buddha of the thousand of this aeon. As sentient beings living during the 5000 year duration of the teachings of Shakyamuni, the fourth of these Buddhas, we have a special relation with Maitreya. Moreover,

Their Holinesses the First and Second Dalai Lamas also shared a close bond with Maitreya Buddha. The residence of the Dalai Lamas, the Potala, was named after Maitreya's celestial palace. Thus it is the practice to transfer your consciousness to Tushita Buddha-field.

6. According to the oral tradition explanation, it is dangerous to end your meditation session with your mind visualized outside your body. Therefore at the conclusion of this practice you should bring your consciousness back into your body through the shaft of light and visualize the shaft withdrawn back into Maitreya's heart. In order to ensure that your consciousness does not accidently leave your body or that harmful forces will not take advantage of you, you should envision the aperture at the crown of your head as sealed with a crossed diamond-scepter (vajra, dorje). However, at the moment of death when you actually do transfer your consciousness to Tushita Buddha-field, you should not bring it back to your deceased body. Remain there instead, merged into the heart of Maitreya Buddha.

The Mantric Recitation of Arya Avalokiteshvara

(A Gem to Fulfill all Needs)

by

The Thirteenth Dalai Lama (1876-1933)

Arrange an altar in a quiet and pleasant place and upon it arrange an image of the Eleven-Headed Protector, the exalted Arya Avalokiteshvara, embodiment of the composition of all Buddhas of the ten directions. In front of this arrange the water and sensory offerings, etc. Then fix yourself a comfortable meditational seat and, sitting in an appropriate posture, begin by taking refuge, developing the bodhi-mind, and so forth. The liturgy for this is as follows.

To the Guru I turn for refuge,
To the Buddha I turn for refuge,
To the Dharma I turn for refuge,
To the Sangha I turn for refuge,
To the Meditational Deities of the mandala,
As well as to those in their retinues,
I turn for refuge.
And to the glorious Dharma Protectors,
Possessors of eyes of wisdom, I turn for refuge. (3x)

To the Buddha, the Dharma and the Supreme Community

Until enlightenment I turn for refuge.
By the merit of my practicing the perfections
May Buddhahood be gained for the sake of all. (3x)

May all sentient beings have happiness and its cause;
May they be free from suffering and its cause;
May they never be separated from that happiness which
is beyond misery;
May they abide in that equanimity which is not moved
by attraction to the near or aversion to the far. (3x)

This complete the preliminaries. Now follows the actual body of the practice.

OṂ PADMANTĀ KṚITA HŪṂ PHAṬ
OṂ SVABHĀVA SHUDDHAḤ SARVA DHARMĀḤ
SVABHĀVA SHUDDHO 'HAṂ.

Everything becomes seen in emptiness.
From within the sphere of emptiness
I arise in the form of Arya Avalokiteshvara
Having eleven heads.

My main face is white in color
And is radiant as the full autumn moon;
To its right is a green face
And to its left a red face.

Above this are green, red and white faces
Respectively in the center and to the right and left.
Above this are red, white and green faces,
Again, in the center, and to the right and left.

Above these is an angry black face
With orange hair swirling upwards,
And, above this, the face of Amitabha Buddha,
Lord of the Family, who possesses an ushnisha.

My two main hands are folded at my heart.
The second, third and fourth on the right
Hold a rosary, the mudra of supreme generosity
And a Wheel of Dharma, respectively.

The second, third and fourth arms on the left
Hold a white lotus of eight opened petals,

A flask, and a bow and arrow.

I am standing with my two feet together.
The skin of an antelope covers my left breast.
Brilliant lights radiate from my jewels.
Ornaments and signs of perfection.

The syllable OṂ marks my head,
ĀḤ my throat and HŪṂ my heart.
Lights shine forth from the HŪṂ at my heart,
Summoning the Buddhas and Bodhisattvas
From their natural abodes; JAḤ HŪṂ BAṂ HOḤ
We merge and become inseparably one.

One then makes the water and sensory offerings, together with mantra and mudra, as follows:

OṂ ĀRYA LOKESHVARA SAPARIVĀRA ARGHAṂ (and so forth, until SHABDE) PRATĪCHCHHA HŪṂ SVĀHĀ.

The praise:

The Dharmakaya of Tathagatas past, present and future
Takes form as the compassionate Avalokiteshvara,
Whose wide eyes watch the six realms of living beings
And whose eleven heads pervade the skies:
To he crowned by Amitabha I bow and offer praise.

The visualization for the mantric recitation:

At my heart upon a moon disc
Stands the white syllable HRĪḤ.
It sends out lights into the ten directions
Which make offerings to the Buddhas and Bodhisattvas.

The transforming powers of these holy beings
Are invoked: they come in the form of lights
Which enter my body via my pores, purifying
My body, speech and mind of obscurations.

Once more light rays shine forth.
They touch the beings of the six realms,
Purifying them of spiritual obstructions and
Placing them in the state of the Noble Avalokiteshvara.

Visualizing as described above, recite the long mantra several times and then recite the short mantra as many times as possible.

The long mantra:

> NAMO RATNA TRAYĀYA, NAMAḤ ĀRYA JÑĀNA SĀGARA, VAIROCHANA, BYŪHARA JĀRA, TATHĀ-GATĀYA, ARHATE, SAMYAKSAṂ BUDDHAYA, NAMAḤ SARVA TATHĀGATE BHYAḤ, ARHATE BHYAḤ, SAMYAKSAṂ BUDDHE BHYAḤ, NAMAḤ ĀRYA AVALOKITESHVARĀYA BODHISATTVĀYA, MAHĀ SATTVĀYA, MAHĀ KARUṆIKĀYA, TADYA-THĀ, OṂ DHARA DHARA, DHIRI DHIRI, DHURU DHURU, ITTE VATTE, CHALE CHALE, PRACHALE PRACHALE, KUSUME KUSUME VARE, ILI MILI, JITI JVALAṂ ĀPANĀYE SVĀHĀ.

The six-syllable mantra:

> OṂ MAṆI PADME HŪṂ

Conclude by reciting the hundred-syllable mantra three or seven times:

> OṂ PADMASATTVA SAMAYA (etc).

Now follow the offerings and praise, and the request:

> OṂ ĀRYA LOKESHVARA SAPARIVĀRA ARGHAṂ (and so forth, until SHABDE) PRATĪCHCHHAYE SVĀHĀ.

> The Dharmakaya of Tathagatas past, present and future
> Takes form as the compassionate Avalokiteshvara.
> Whose wide eyes watch the six realms living beings
> And whose eleven heads pervade the skies:
> To he crowned by Amitabha I bow and offer praise.
>
> O Arya Avalokiteshvara, treasure of compassion,
> And also, O deities of your retinue,
> Pray, grant be your attention.
>
> Quickly liberate from the ocean of samsara
> Myself and all the parent-like sentient beings
> Who are languishing in the six realms.

Quickly give birth within my mindstream
To both the vast and profound bodhi-minds.
To great compassion combined with wisdom of the
ultimate.

With the soothing waters of your compassion
Quickly wash away all our mental distortions
And negative karmas collected since beginningless time.

O Gently Gazing Bodhisattva,
Stretch out your hand of compassion
And lead myself and all others
To Sukhavati, the Pure Land of Bliss.

In life upon life may I be befriended
By Amitabha Buddha and Avalokiteshvara;
May they lead me along the unmistaken path
And quickly place me on the ground of Buddhahood.

By the meritorious energy of this practice
May I quickly gain the state of Avalokiteshvara;
And may all beings without exception
Be then led to that very same state.

Once more recite the hundred-syllable mantra:

OṂ PADMA SATTVA SAMAYA (etc).

O Compassionate One, for anything herein done wrong
Due to ignorance, lack of materials or inability.
O Bodhisattva, I beg you to be forbearing
With all of these mistakes.

The conclusion:

The Wisdom Beings,
Pleased with my practice,
Dissolve into me.
I myself dissolve into emptiness
And then reappear as Arya Avalokiteshvara.

The dedication:

May goodness reign during the day;
May goodness reign during the night.
May goodness reign throughout the day and night

And may there constantly be the auspicious signs
Of the prosperity of the Three Jewels of Refuge.

The colophon: Written by the Buddhist practitioner Thubten Gyatso at the repeated request of the temple servant Yeshe Damcho.

Translated into English by Glenn H. Mullin with Chomdze Tashi Wangyal.

The Fasting Practice of Eleven-Faced Avalokiteshvara

by

The Fifth Dalai Lama (1617-1682)

For the benefit of beginners, I shall expand a few points
From the corpus of rituals relating to the fast,
Which come from the textual critique of the highly-
realized Bhikshuni Lakshmi,
Who was cared for by the Bearer of the White Lotus.

It is the practice of the living lineage to have the following prerequisites: a mandala; representations of the Enlightened, One's Body, Speech and Mind; a vase for the ritual; and so on.

The actual practice is divided into the preliminaries, the main body and the conclusion.

(1. Preliminaries:)

Recite:

OṂ PADMA UDBHĀVAYE SVĀHĀ

Accompany this recitation with the (appropriate) gesture of the hands, then wash (the five points on the body).

(The ordination:)

If one takes the vows in the presence of a spiritual master, it follows that one will necessarily receive them from him. If they are taken before the altar, one should prostrate and imagine one is receiving them from the Great Compassionate One, who is in fact the spiritual master, encircled by Buddhas and Bodhisattvas.

(Symbolic offering of the universe:)

OṂ VAJRA BHŪMI ĀḤ HŪṂ. Here is the mighty and massive

golden base. OṂ VAJRA REKHE ĀḤ HŪṂ. Here is the adamantine fence. The outer ring is encircled by the iron fence, in the center of which is the towering pinnacle Meru—king of mountains. In the east is the Continent of Giants, in the south, the Continent of Rose-apples, in the west, the continent of Cow Husbandry, in the north, the Continent of the Voice of Doom. To the east, the... sub-continents of Huge and Colossal, to the south, those of Cannibals and Non-cannibals, to the west, those of Trickery and Travelling the Excellent Path, to the north, those of Cheerless Voice and Distressing Sound. In the east is the precious mountain, in the south, the wish-granting tree, in the west, the wish-fulfilling cow, in the north the harvest that requires no cultivation.

Here is the precious wheel, the precious jewel, the precious queen, the precious minister, the precious elephant, the precious and excellent horse, the precious general and the great treasure-vase. Here is the beauty goddess, the garland goddess, the song goddess, the dance goddess, the flower goddess, the incense goddess, the illumination goddess and the perfume goddess. Here is the sun, the moon, the precious umbrella and the banner of total victory in all directions. In the center is the entire wealth of gods and men. I offer infinite numbers of this stainless and captivating panoply, complete in every respect, to you my most kind root Master, as well as to all excellent and illustrious Lineage Masters; I offer them particularly to you, Lama Je Tzong Khapa, to you, the Buddha, and to you, the Great Vajra Holder, as well as to the retinues and hosts of gods.

Out of your great compassion, please accept this for the sake of wandering beings and, having done so, with loving compassion please bless and inspire me and all motherly sentient beings who are illimitable like space itself.

> I offer this fragrant flower-strewn vase,
> Adorned with the soaring pinnacle, the four continents,
>   the sun and moon
> Visualized as a Buddha-field;
> And may all wandering beings share the intrinsic
>   goodness.

> Only by the kindness of my Master have I met
> With the doctrine of this Guide who is without peer;
> I dedicate this merit, that all wandering beings
> May be cared for by Mentors most sublime.

OṂ IDAM GURU RATṆA MAṆḌALAKAṂ NIRYATA-YĀMI. I send forth this jewelled mandala to you, precious Teachers.

(The ordination ceremony:)

Repeat the following after the Master, or (in his absence) with whomever is the preceptor.

Previous Blessed Ones, Liberated Ones and fully enlightened Beings, such as Excellent Horse and Great Elephant, did all that was necessary, accomplished all tasks, shed the burden (of the contaminated five aggregates), fulfilled their aspirations, and, while living in cyclic existence, have utterly destroyed innate self-grasping. Their speech is perfection; their minds are sublime transcendence; they possess the transcendental wisdom understanding emptiness. They utilized these qualities for the welfare of all sentient beings: in order to serve them, in order to liberate them, in order to prevent famine, in order to eradicate sickness, in order to fully consummate the (thirty-seven) wings to enlightenment, and in order to incontrovertibly realize the peerless and perfect finality of enlightenment. So I too, whose name is......., will scrupulously maintain the ordination from now until sunrise tomorrow. (3x)

(The precepts:)

Henceforth neither will I kill,
Nor steal others' things,
Nor indulge in any sex,
Nor speak untrue words.
Intoxicants will I truly shun,
Large, high beds and thrones I will not use,
Nor eat at proscribed times;
Perfumes, rosaries and ornaments I shall not wear;
Singing, dancing and so forth I shall avoid.
Just as the Liberated Ones never engage
In such actions as taking life,
I likewise shall give up killing.
Peerless enlightenment may I quickly gain.
May those of the world plagued by many woes
Be freed from the ocean-vast cycle of lives. (IX)

(Recite the mantra twenty-one times for keeping the precepts pure:)

OṂ AMOGHA SHĪLA SAMBHARA, BHARA BHARA, MAHĀ SHUDDHA SATTVA PADMA BIBHUSHITA BHUJA, DHARA DHARA, SAMANTA, AVALOKITE HŪM PHAṬ SVĀHĀ. (21X)

(Next bless the offerings by three recitations of:)

OṂ SARVAVID PŪRA PŪRA, SŪRA SŪRA, AVARTAYA AVARTAYA HO, VAJRAS PHARṆAYAṂ (3X)

(Taking refuge and generation of the altruistic mind of enlightenment:)

I take refuge in the Buddha, I take refuge in the Teachings, and I take refuge in the Supreme Community until I gain enlightenment. By the virtue I gather from practicing giving and the other perfections, may I attain Buddhahood in order to benefit all sentient beings. (3X)

(The field of merit:)

Visualizing myself as the Great Compassionate One, light rays from my heart invite the entire field of merit. "Please come here before me!"

However little merit I have accumulated from
Prostration, offering, admission,
Rejoicing, requesting, and exhorting,
I dedicate it all towards the finality of enlightenment.

The various non-virtues and defilements which I
Have accumulated in my many lives up till now,
I sincerely acknowledge with remorse and shall exercise restraint.
By dint of the four powers, may they be cleaned and purified.

(The actual practice, Self-generation:)

OṂ SVABHĀVA SHUDDHAḤ SARVA DHARMĀḤ SVABHĀVA SHUDDHOḤ 'HAṂ

All phenomena become emptiness. Within the sphere of emptiness appears the syllable PAṂ which becomes a lotus. (On it) is the syllable ĀḤ which becomes a moon-disc upon which is a white syllable HŪṂ, which transforms. Thus I emerge as the eleven-faced Great Compassionate One.

My central face is white, the one to its right is green and the one to its left is red; a further central face is on top of these three. It is green, with a red face to its right, and a white face to its left. On top of these is a central red face, a white face to its right, and a green one to its left. On top of these is a wrathful black face, above which is a serene red face having a crown protrusion.

My first pair of hands are clasped at my heart. The right of my second pair holds a rosary, while the left holds a lotus. My third right hand is in the gesture of giving protection, my third left hand holds a spouted vase. My fourth pair hold a wheel and a bow-and-arrow; the remaining nine hundred and ninety-two hands, each with an eye in the palm, are all in the gesture of giving protection.

I stand upright with both feet placed together, and am wearing silken raiment and precious ornaments. OṂ marks my forehead, ĀḤ my throat, and HŪṂ my heart. The HŪṂ at my heart emits rays of light to invite the Wisdom Being who resembles my own visualized form. I ask him, "Please come to the space before me!"

JAḤ HŪṂ BAṂ HOḤ (we merge into one).

Once more light pours forth from the seed syllable at my heart to invite the five Dhyani Buddhas with their retinues. I ask them, "Please come to the space before me! Please will you all bestow initiation on me!" Because of this entreaty, they confer the initiation with the waters from their vases, filling my body and purifying all imperfections. The excess liquid swirls into a crown protrusion, which transforms into the five Dhyani Buddhas adorning my head.

Upon the moon-disc at my heart is a white Wisdom Being with one face and two arms. At this heart, on a moon cushion, is a white HŪṂ—the Concentration Being—surrounded at the edge of the moon by the six syllables. (Contemplate this whilst reciting the mantra OṂ MAṆI PADME HŪṂ.)

(Front-generation:)

OṂ SVABHĀVA SHUDDHAḤ SARVA DHARMĀḤ
SVABHĀVA SHUDDHOḤ 'HAṂ

From the seed syllable at my heart, yet while still within the sphere of emptiness, goes forth a white syllable BHRŪṂ to the space before me. It transforms into a jewelled inconceivable mansion complete in all respects. At its center is a precious throne, on which is a white HRĪḤ on a lotus cushion. HRĪḤ transforms into the eleven-faced Great Compassionate One. His central face is white, the one to its right is green and the one to its left is red; a further central face is on top of these. It is green, with a red face to its right, and a white face to its left. On top of these is a red central face, with a white face to its right, and a green one to its left. On top of these is a wrathful black face, above which is a serene red face having a crown protrusion.

His first pair of hands are clasped at the heart. The right of his second pair holds a rosary, while the left holds a lotus. His third right hand is in the gesture of giving protection, the third left hand holds a spouted vase. The fourth pair hold a wheel and a bow-and-arrow, the remaining nine hundred and ninety-two hands, each with an eye in the palm, are all in the gesture of giving protection. He stands erect with both feet placed together, and is wearing silken raiment and precious ornaments.

From HŪṂ in the east appears Akshobhya, from TRAṂ in the south, Ratnasambhava, from OṂ in the west, Vairochana, from ĀḤ in the north, Amoghasiddhi, each in his own color and hand gestures.

Light pours forth from the seed syllable at his heart to invite the five Dhyani Buddhas with their retinues. "Please come to the space before me! Please, all of you, bestow initiation on me!" Because of this entreaty, they confer the initiation with the waters from their vases which fill his body purifying all imperfections. The excess liquid swirls into a crown protrusion, which transforms into the five Dhyani Buddhas adorning his head.

(The offerings:)

> OṂ SARVA TATHĀGATA LOKESHVARA SAPARI-VĀRA ARGHAṂ (and so on till SHABDE) PRATĪCH-CHHA HŪṂ SVĀHĀ

(A praise:)

> White in color and untarnished by faults,
> The Buddha Amitabha embellishing the crown of your head,
> You gaze upon sentient beings with overwhelming compassion,
> To Avalokiteshvara I humbly bow down.

Streams of nectar pour forth from both my own fingers, and those of Avalokiteshvara before me, filling the altar vase with the waters of wisdom.

(Having contemplated in this way, recite the six syllables as many times as possible.)

(3. Conclusion of the ritual. Further entreaties:)

O compassionate Bodhisattva, stretch forth your hand;
and in due course
Convey myself and all others to Sukhavati, realm of bliss!
May the invaluable spiritual guide of all my myriad lives
Bless me, that I may soon achieve the state of a Buddha!

(Ritual cake offering:)

OṂ ĀḤ HŪṂ blesses the ritual cake.

OṂ ĀRYA LOKESHVARA SAPARIVĀRA BALIṂ PRATĪCHCHHAYE SVĀHĀ. (3X)

(Recite this three times, while offering to the Superior Avalokiteshvara.)

OṂ AKHAROMUKHAṂ SARVA DHARMĀNĀṂ ADHYANUTPAN NATVAD OṂ ĀḤ HŪṂ PHAṬ SVĀHĀ. (3X)

(Recite this three times, while offering to the protectors and local spirits.)

(Ritual ablution of the deity, and an entreaty:)

This is made using the water from the altar vase, which is poured on the reflection of the deity appearing in the ritual mirror.

By offering ablution with a stream of fragrant nectar
To the protector Avalokiteshvara, the light of wandering
beings,
May the two obscurations and all imperfections of beings
be removed.
And may good omen favor their attainment of the three
untainted kayas.

Avalokiteshvara, forgive all my errors (and omissions herein); may my practice never slacken.

With the recitation of OṂ MAṆI PADME HŪṂ, the Superior (Avalokiteshvara) comes in the space before me; and due to the ablution and entreaty, I feel that both my obscurations are purified. I taste the nectar from the vase.

When I go to sleep, I visualize myself as the Commitment Being deity-form. This absorbs into the Wisdom Being. He dissolves into the concentration Being. This in turn dissolves into non-objectifying (meditative equipoise). With such a contem-plation, I go to sleep.

These practices, especially those relating to the fasting and eating days, should be carried out in accordance with the practice of the living lineage and those in other textbooks. At the end of (a two-day) fast, after dawn on the sixteenth day of the Tibetan month, perform the ritual once, omitting the ordination ceremony section. Then:

OṂ SUPRATIṢHTHA VAJRAYE SVĀHĀ

May the Wisdom Being stay and dwell in the mandala visualized before me!

VAJRA MUḤ. The set of deities leave for their own abodes.

(The auspicious verse:)

May the day be auspicious, as well as the night,
And may good omen favor noontide too;
May the auspicious nature of the Three Jewels
Ever be favorable, for time without end.

The colophon:

In spite of my heartfelt, fervent regard,
I am oppressed by the manifold burden
Or vacillation caused by worldly concerns;
So, how wonderful that the potency
Of a mere drop from this ocean of nectar
Will ensure the immortality of perpetual bliss.

This was composed by Ngagwang Lozang Gyatso, a venerable monk of Zahor, at the insistence of King Tenzin Dahyen who, by virtue of his formidable power, holds sway over all the earth mandalas. He pointed out the need for such an extremely practical text on the gist of fasting practice. It was taken down by my scribe, Nayben Jamyang.

Translated by Kevin Garratt, Chomdze Tashi Wangyal and Yeshe Lodro Rinpoche.

Brief Notes on the Fasting Practice

by

The Fifth Dalai Lama (1617-1682)

I bow down to the highly-realized Bhikshuni Lakshmi,
Who was personally guided by the Bearer of the White Lotus,
And I will set forth this brief outline of the fasting practice
In accordance with the experience of that mighty yogini

This particular tradition of the fasting practice, so well-known in India and Tibet, has an extensive lineage (starting) from the fully ordained nun, Lakshmi, who was under the protection of the Great Compassionate One, Avalokiteshvara. Many scholars, especially here in Tibet, have still maintained an unbroken continuity of this practice. One need only regard the many authentic textbooks written by such erudite people as Sonam Zangpo, the Nyambern Rinpoche.

However, in times like these, there are teachers with little study and contemplation into the scriptures of the teachers of old, and who have not mastered the teachings of the sutras and tantras. There are many such haughty fools who, motivated by profit, act as preceptors in the fasting rite. Here they mistake the introductory verses of the rite with those of the One-day Pratimoksha vow. One of these verses ends with "....from now on until tomorrow morning," while the other begins with "Henceforth I will neither kill...." Because the eight things to be abandoned (stated in these verses) in the fasting rite are similar to those pertaining to the One-day Pratimoksha Vow, these foolish teachers confuse the meaning of the two, and on each of the eight days of fasting confer the One-day Pratimoksha Vow. They even call these days the Pratimoksha Days. This is incorrect.

To look at the two etymologies: the One-day Vow is said to be for the ordinary person who is unable to be without attachment and gross behavior; that it brings the ordinary person the means of being without these two faults. The meaning of the words One-day Vow is that, for a day, an ordinary person is brought in proximity to Arhatship; and , also, that for one day, he gains a taste of the lifelong Pratimoksha vows (such as those of the monkhood, etc.).

On the other hand, the Fasting Vow refers not merely to the avoidance of these eight things (as in the One-day Vow). On each of the days of total fast, one is not allowed to swallow even one's own spittle. This is the meaning of the word "fasting".

Further, the One-day Pratimoksha Vow is a type of vow that can only be held by a layman. As it is one of the eight types of Pratimoksha Vow, it is therefore taken only with renunciation serving as its basis. It does not require the generation of the altruistic mind of enlightenment. One only gives up eight things for a day; any other recitations, virtuous activities, and so on, are purely optional. These are no other rules laid down, and no special mention made about one's doing any tantric rituals or recitations.

The precepts taken during the fasting retreat are in the Mahayana tradition; so it is necessary to generate the altruistic mind of enlightenment. One must also perform the front-and self-generation rituals of Avalokiteshvara three times each, on both the days of fasting and on those when you may take food. This is explained in reliable textbooks, and is also the standard practice.

One should, therefore, make a thorough investigation and treat with skepticism any tradition that makes no distinction between sutra and tantra, or between Mahayana and Hinayana. One should be critical. These propounders of a false type of fasting retreat are people you should ignore, because they have exceeded the bounds of sober, objective analysis. They (are the type of people), who, upon surveying the suffering of the six types of beings, would then proceed to count radishes as things having minds.

Those wishing to actually engage in the fasting practice should ideally have received the empowerment for Eleven-faced Avalokiteshvara. The next best is to have a detailed initiation into this particular tradition. Failing these, an initiation into (any of the traditions of) the eleven-faced deity will suffice.

It is best to begin in the fourth Tibetan month. Otherwise, (in the case of a two-day fast) start at first light on either the fourteenth or twenty-ninth of any Tibetan month.

Set up a statue or scroll painting of the eleven-faced One and lay out some splendid offerings. In front of these, your preceptor, who should previously have bathed himself and cleaned the room, conducts the general preliminaries: taking refuge according to either the short or long formulas, and the generation of the altruistic mind of enlightenment. The ordination is received upon the third repetition of the Mahayana Ordination section of the ritual. Recite the verses starting with the line "Henceforth I will neither kill...." once, as well as repeating twenty-one times the mantra (for keeping) the precept pure.

The preceptor should take his place on a high seat. The disciples make three prostrations to him, after which they should sit facing him. The preceptor should give a detailed or brief explanation of the salient features and benefits of this preliminary practice. (He then conducts the ceremony and lists the vows). The disciples should repeat these after him in response. On the following mornings, the disciples may take the ordination alone before the altar. The presence of the preceptor is not required.

Consult the writings of such eminent scholars as the omniscient Gendun Gyatso and Nyambern Rinpoche for all practical details to do with curtailing one's food intake; how to apply one's mind (in general); and for details concerning the front—and self-generation rituals.

The colophon: This elaborate outline of the salient points to the practice of fasting was composed by the venerable monk of Zahor (the Fifth Dalai Lama), at the request of Lochok Rigpay Dorjay, both a scholar and adept in the five major sciences generally, and a particular authority on the treasury of the Buddha's speech enshrined in tantric texts of the earlier Nyingma translation period. This outline was taken down by the author's scribe, Jamyang Tenzin.

CHAPTER FOUR

MANJUSHRI, THE BODHISATTVA OF WISDOM

A Meditation Upon Orange Manjushri

by

The Fifth Dalai Lama (1617-1682)

NAMO GURUJA VĀGĪḤ SHARAHYA.

I make humble obeisance to you, great Tzong Khapa,
Personification of Manjushri in human form with all the marks and signs of perfection.
Your magnificent attainments were nurtured in the matrix of motherly method and Wisdom combined
Of which the vibrant syllable BHĪḤ is an embodiment.
Sipping the nectars of the profound teachings,
Directly from Manjushri's masterly eloquence,
You realized the heart of wisdom.
Inspired by your example, I will now set out
A description of the steps for actualization
Of Manjushri, the Bodhisattva of wisdom,
In accord with your realization.

(Begin the session with the general preliminaries of taking refuge and generating the altruistic thought of enlightenment. Then contemplate the four immeasurable thoughts of love, compassion, joy and equanimity. Recite the Svabhava mantra to purify perception in emptiness and then proceed as follows:)

At my heart is my mind in the shape of an egg, its point upwards. Inside the egg on a full moon disc is an orange letter DHĪḤ, from which an infinite amount of light emits. It fills the whole of my body, purifying all my negativities and removing all my obscurations accumulated since beginningless time. The light rays then leave through my pores and become offerings to the Buddhas and Bodhisattvas. The lights then become offerings for the Buddhas and Bodhisattvas, thereby delighting them. This causes the blessings of the body, speech and mind of these holy beings to dissolve into light that destroys the darkness of ignorance of all sentient beings, thus placing them in wisdom's illumination.

The rays then recollect into the syllable DHĪḤ. It transforms into light, my ordinary perception and my clinging thereto vanish, and I emerge as the Venerable Manjushri, orange in color, with one face and two arms.

My right hand brandishes a Sword of Wisdom in the space above me. At my heart between the thumb and ring finger of my left hand I hold the stem of an utpala lotus. Upon its petals in full bloom by my left ear rests a volume of the *Perfection of Wisdom Sutra*. I sit in full lotus posture and am adorned with precious ornaments for my head, ears, throat and shoulders, as well as bracelets and anklets. Draped in a flowing mantle and skirt of exquisite silks, my hair is tied up in five knots and coils anticlockwise. Bearing an entrancing and serene smile, I sit amidst a mass of light radiating from my body. The letter OṂ marks the crown of my head, ĀḤ my throat, and HŪṂ my heart.

HŪṂ emits rays of light that invite the Wisdom Beings from the inconceivable mansion of their own pure lands. They resemble the Manjushri described above and are surrounded by hosts of Buddhas and Bodhisattvas.

JAḤ HŪṂ BAṂ HOḤ: They absorb into me and thus we become one.

(One then makes the offerings and praise:)

> OṂ ĀRYA VĀGĪḤ SHARA SAPARIVĀRA ARGHAṂ (and so forth, until SHABDE) PRATĪCHCHHA HŪṂ SVĀHĀ.

I make obeisance to your youthful form, O Manjushri,
Like that of a dynamic and graceful sixteen year old.
You repose upon the full moon as your cushion
At the center of an expansive, milk-white lotus.
I make obeisance to your speech, O mighty Fulfiller of Wishes,
So mellifluent to the minds of countless sentient beings,
A lucent euphony to accord with each listener's capacity,
Its multiplicity embellishing the hearing of all fortunate ones.

O Manjushri, I make obeisance to your mind
Wherein is illuminated the entire tapestry of the myriad objects of knowledge
It is a tranquil ocean of unfathomable profundity
Of immeasurable breadth, boundless like space itself.

(The mantra recitation:)

At my heart upon a moon disc is an orange syllable DHĪḤ. Encircling it at the disc's periphery stands the rosary-like mantra of OM AH RA PA TZA NA. All the syllables radiate light, which gathers both the wisdoms of hearing, contemplation and meditation, which are possessed by the Buddhas, Bodhisattvas, Sravakas, Pratyekabuddhas, and the wise and learned masters of all the Buddhist and non-Buddhist traditions.

(One contemplates the fusion of such wisdom within one's mindstream and recites the mantra accordingly. Conclude the session with the hundred syllable Vajrasattva mantra to purify excesses, omissions and mistakes. Then end with some prayers and auspicious verses:)

By the virtue of this practice may I quickly
Accomplish the powerful attainments of Manjushri;
And then may I lead all beings without exception
To that same supreme state.

The colophon: The above meditation upon Orange Manjushri was written by Ngawang Lozang Gyatso, a monk of rectitude from Zahor, at the request of Gajo Dargye.

Translated by Kevin Garratt with Chomdze Tashi Wangyal and Lozang Gyaltsen.

A White Manjushri Method

by

The Second Dalai Lama (1475-1542)

(The ritual begins with the usual preliminaries of taking refuge and developing the altruistic thought of enlightenment. Then follows the incantation of the formula to correct one's mental perception:)

OṂ SVABHĀVA SHUDDHOḤ SARVA DHARMĀḤ SVABHĀVA SHUDDHO 'HAṂ. All becomes seen as emptiness. Within the sphere of emptiness appears the syllable BAṂ. BAṂ becomes an enormous lotus-strewn expanse of pure and perfect milk. It is encompassed by verdant pastures where browse many white elephants having six tusks. At the center of the lotus stands the syllable ĀṂ, which transforms into a mollifying white moon disc. Upon that is my own mind in the form of a flawless white syllable ĀḤ. Light emanates from this letter and becomes offerings for all the Buddhas and Bodhisattvas. The light also destroys the nescient darkness of all sentient beings, who thereby gain wisdom's illumination.

The light re-collects into the ĀḤ, which transforms, and I emerge as the Venerable Manjushri of luminescent white hue like that of the autumn moon. I have one face and two arms. My right hand, in the gesture of giving protection, holds the stem of a white lotus which blooms beside my right ear. Upon its petals is the sword of wisdom. My left hand, in the teaching gesture, holds at my heart the stem of a white lotus which opens in full bloom beside my left ear. Upon this lotus is a volume of the *Perfection of Wisdom Sutra*. I am clad in an array of silks, am adorned by precious ornaments and sit with an entrancing smile, my legs locked in the full lotus posture, radiant with the vigor of a sixteen year old youth. The syllable OṂ marks the crown of my head, ĀḤ my throat and HŪṂ my heart.

HŪṂ emits rays which invite the Venerable Manjushri and retinue of Buddhas and Bodhisattvas from their own abodes. JAḤ HŪṂ BAṂ HOḤ: They absorb into me and we become one. Once again lights emanate from the HŪṂ at my heart, inviting the Empowering Deities. "Please grant me initiation." They raise aloft vases brimming with wisdom nectar: OṂ SARVA TATHĀ-GATAYA ABHIṢHEKATA SAMAYA SHRĪYE HŪṂ. They initiate me with their nectar, which completely fills my body and purifies me of all defilements. The excess nectar on the crown of my head transforms into the Buddha Akshobya who becomes my crown ornament.

(Offerings to clear interferences, purify and receive blessings:)

> OṂ ĀRYA MAÑJUSHRĪ SAPARIVĀRA ARGHAṂ (and so forth, until SHABDE) PRATĪCHCHHAYE SVĀHĀ

(Now offer verses of praise:)

> I make humble obeisance to you, Manjushri,
> Great destroyer of mistaken perception.
> Wide like the lotus petal are your eyes,
> Your mind the pinnacle of expansive bliss.
> Your body resplendently white as the effulgent moon,
> A sword of Wisdom and Holy Writ in hand,
> Your hair coiled in five knots: thus you
> Epitomize the splendor and tranquility of eternal youth.

(The mantra recitation:)

At my heart is a white wheel consisting of hub, six spokes and rim. On the hub is a moon disc upon which is my own mind in the form of a syllable ĀḤ. On the six spokes respectively stand the six white syllables OṂ VĀKYE DAMNAMAH in capital letters. They are glitteringly white like the soothing radiance of autumnal moonlight. An infinite amount of light comes forth from them, filling my whole body and dispelling all the nescient darkness enveloping my body, speech and mind.

(Regarding the detailed contemplation in order to gain a perfect grasp of profound discrimination like that of Manjushri, recite the mantra silently while concentrating on the clockwise rotation of the wheel and the anticlockwise rotation of the six syllables. By reciting the mantra in this way twenty or thirty thousand times in each session, an excellent discriminating wisdom is quickly achieved. Feel assured that a complete recollection of the meaning of all the scriptural categories, without any relapse of memory, has been gained. Conclude the session with peerless dedications of merit and heartfelt prayers. (If desired, end the evening session by offering a ritual cake. Place a white ritual cake in a vessel, which may be of precious substance. Sprinkle a little of the inner offering and recite the following mantra to clear interferences:)

OṂ VAJRA KUNḌALI HANA MANA HŪṂ PHAṬ

(Then to correct mental perception:)

OṂ SVABHĀVA SHUDDAH SARVA DHARMĀḤ SVABHĀVA SHUDDOḤ'HAṂ. By nature everything is emptiness. Within the sphere of emptiness appears the syllable OṂ which becomes a precious vessel as vast as the three realms. Within it are the syllables OṂ ĀḤ HŪṂ. These melt into light and become a colossal expanse of superlative ritual cake nectar.

OṂ ĀḤ HŪṂ (3X)

In the sphere before me appears a Manjushri, the Omniscient Being, who is an exact replica of my own visualized form. To you, O Manjushri, I offer thus:

OṂ ĀRYA MAÑJUSHRĪ SAPARIVĀRA ARGHAṂ (and so forth, until SHABDE) PRATĪCHCHHAYE SVĀHĀ.

The syllable HŪṂ on the tongue of this guest becomes a single spoked white vajra. Extending from this vajra is a hollow beam of light which enables him to imbibe the nectar's essence.

> OṂ ĀRYA MAÑJUSHRĪ SAPARIVĀRA IDAM BALIMTA KHA KHA KHĀHI KHĀHI.

One recites this mantra seven times. Then make outer offerings and praises as before. Finally conclude with similar dedication of merit and prayers as used in the other sessions.

Between sessions, put great effort into purification of non-virtue and accumulation of merit as well as offering praises and reciting the names of the many Buddhas. When making retreat, be scrupulous in observing the lower tantra practices of washing and general cleanliness. Integrate all daily activities into the practice.

(The use of a pea to gauge success in the retreat:)

Upon completion of the required number of mantra recitations in the retreat, do as follows. Soak a germinative lentil in a mixture of fragrant water and milk from a red cow. Thereafter wrap it neatly in white silk. At the start of a solar or lunar eclipse place it under your tongue and recite the mantra silently for the complete duration of the eclipse. The appearance of a sprout may be taken as a sign of accomplishment.

(How to gain supremacy in disputation:)

Whether engaging in debate or in mere argument, establish clear self-identification as White Manjushri. At the thumb tip of your right hand, in the gesture of granting protection, is a pointed sword. Upon the sword handle is a white syllable ĀḤ that emanates light, drawing into itself the opponent's cunning in the way a magnet attracts iron. The light, thus charged, returns and dissolves into the ĀḤ. Hence your opponents wisdom now augments your own. One also visualizes that the flames at the sword's tip shoot out and scorch the opponents' tongue. When the mantra is recited in conjunction with these visualizations, one will certainly gain the ability to vanquish all adversaries.

The colophon: This ritual of White Manjushri was composed by Gyalwa Gendun Gyatso.

Translated into English by Kevin Garratt with Tashi Wangyal and Lozang Gyaltsen.

CHAPTER FIVE

Arya Tara, Source of Enlightened Energy

The Longevity Method of White Tara

(The Wish-Fulfilling Wheel)

by

The Seventh Dalai Lama (1708-1757)

In a pleasant and harmonious place, arrange an altar with an image of White Tara, the Wish Fulfilling Wheel, in the center. Before her arrange two rows of offering bowls, to be offered to the deities visualized in front and to yourself as the deity. As well, arrange the white ritual cake made of three sweet and three white substances, in accordance with lower tantra tradition. If making the full retreat, be sure to observe the various commitments of Kriya Tantra, such as washing and so forth, and abstain from black foods such as meat, garlic, onions, radishes, etc.

The *sadhana* has three phases: the preliminaries, the actual practice and the conclusion.

(Firstly, preliminaries. This refers to the general meditations of taking refuge and generating the bodhi-mind. The liturgy for this is as follows:)

Visualizing myself as White Tara, I emanate lights from the letter TAṂ at my heart. Tara, crowned by Buddha Amitabha and surrounded by myriads of Buddhas and Bodhisattvas, is invited from her natural abode to the skies before me. NAMO GURU BYAḤ NAMA ĀRYĀ TĀRE SAPARIVĀRA BYAḤ.

(One then makes the mudra of prostration, performs the outer offerings and chants the praise. Then take refuge, generate the bodhi-mind and contemplate the four immeasurables in accordance with the standard verses.

When this has been accomplished, one should proceed with the actual body of the meditation. This begins by purifying the meditation in emptiness realization by means of the Svabhava mantra:)

OṂ SVABHĀVA SHUDDHOḤ SARVA DHARMĀḤ SVABHĀVA SHUDDHO 'HAM. All Dharmas, empty of self existence, melt into emptiness. From within the sphere of this vast expanse of voidness there appears a letter PAM. It transforms into a white lotus bearing a letter Āh. Āh transforms into a moon disc, at the center of which is my own mind in the form of a white letter TAṂ.

TAṂ emits lights, which make offerings to the High Ones, work the good of sentient beings and then re-collect. The letter TAṂ transforms completely and I emerge as exalted White Tara, the Wish Fulfilling Wheel.

My body is white in color and has one face and two arms. It is as vibrant as that of a sixteen year old youth of great beauty. My right hand is in the mudra of supreme generosity, my left at my heart, the stem of a white lotus held between the thumb and ring finger. To symbolize the Buddhas of the three times, the lotus spreads into three branches beside my ear. The middle branch bears a flower in full bloom; the right, one that has gone to fruit; and the left, an unopened bud. My hair is tied up in a knot, I am adorned with the various jewelled ornaments and am clothed in silken garments. My back rests upon a moon disc, my entire body is of the nature of light, and my feet are in the vajra posture. White OṂ marks the crown of my head, red ĀḤ my throat and blue HŪṂ my heart. As well, a white letter TAṂ rests upon a moon disc at my heart.

TAṂ emits beams of light, inviting exalted Tara, who is surrounded by masses of Buddhas and Bodhisattvas, from her natural abode: JAḤ HŪṂ BAṂ HOḤ. We merge to become non-dual.

Again lights proceed from the letter TAṂ at my heart, inviting the Empowering Deities. I request them, "Pray, bestow initiation upon me."

Thus requested, they hold up vases filled with nectars of wisdom. OṂ SARVA TATHĀGATA SAMAYA SHRĪYE ĀḤ HŪṂ. Saying this, they initiate me with their ambrosial waters. My body becomes filled with ambrosia and I am cleansed of all negativities. The surplus ambrosia that overflows the crown of my head transforms into Amitabha who becomes my crown ornament.

(Making offerings to oneself as the deity:)

OṂ SVABHĀVA SHUDDAH SARVA DHARMĀḤ
SVABHĀVA SHUDDHO 'HAM!

Everything becomes (seen as) emptiness. From the sphere of emptiness appear eight letters OṂ, which transform into huge, vast, jewelled containers, inside each of which is an OṂ. The letters OṂ melt into light and reappear in the form of the offering substances: water for the mouth, water for the feet, flowers, incense, light, scented oil, food and music. These are all pure and equal to the limits of the sky.

OṂ ARGHAṂ ĀH HŪṂ (and so forth, until SHABDE).
(This consecrates them. Then make the offering:)

OṂ ĀRYĀ TĀRE SAPARIVĀRA ARGHAṂ PRATĪCHCHHA HŪṂ SVĀHĀ, OṂ ĀRYA TĀRE SAPARIVĀRA, PĀDYAM (etc., for) PUṢPE, DHUPE, ĀLOKE, GANDHE NAIVIDYE, SHABDA—PRATĪ-CHCHHA HŪṂ SVĀHĀ.

TĀRE means freedom from samsara; TUTTĀRE, freedom from the eight terrors; TURE, freedom from illness; homage to mother Tara.

Homage to the Supremely Generous One who sits in the vajra posture on a moon disc at the heart of a white lotus.

Homage to she radiant as the autumn moon, her back resting upon a moon disc, her body made beautiful with ornaments, her left hand holding a white lotus.

Homage to Arya Tara, who appears as a sixteen-year-old youth, mother of all Buddhas, she whose form spontaneously fulfills wishes.

Homage to she with a white wheel at her heart, a wheel with eight spokes bearing eight mystic letters and blazing forth lights.

Exalted Tara, mother who brings liberation, Wish-Fulfilling Wheel increasing life; hear this prayer of mine. Protect me from dangers to my life, and from sickness and misery. Bestow upon me the supreme siddhi of realization and the common siddhis as well. High and exalted one in whom I place faith, care for me always as a mother for her child. I call to you: catch me on your hook of compassion. Transcended goddess white as the autumn moon, perfect one haughty yet serene, she beautified with jewelled ornaments, clothed in silks and sitting in the vajra posture upon a lotus and moon, having a smiling face and two arms, mother of Buddhas past, present and future, repeatedly I bow down to you. Pray, be moved by my devotion and help me to accomplish enlightenment. From now until I attain bodhi, pacify all negative circumstances that may hinder me. Make flourish every circumstance conducive and helpful. (This praise and request was written by the First Dalai Lama.)

At my heart appears a white wheel, having eight spokes, a hub and a three-layered rim. At the hub is a white moon disc and upon it stands my own mind in the form of a white letter TAṂ.

Encircling the TAṂ is the mantra OṂ MAMĀ ĀYUH PUṆYE JṆĀNA PUṢHṬHIM KURU SVĀHĀ. Upon the spokes, beginning in front and circling clockwise, are the letters TĀRE TUTTĀRE TURE SVĀ.

On the inner layer of the rim of the wheel, the sixteen vowels of the Sanskrit alphabet, white in color, circle counter-clockwise. On the middle layer the thirty-four consonants, red in color, circle clockwise. And on the outside layer is the mantra called "The Essence of Relativity", blue in color, circling clockwise: OṂ YE DHARMA HETU PRABHĀVA HETUN TEṢHĀN TATHĀGATO HYA VADATA TEṢHĀN CHAYO NIRODHA EVAṂ VĀDI MAHĀSHRAMAṆAH YE SVĀHĀ. All these letters are in large block letters, stand upright and radiate an infinite quantity of light.

From them come white lights equal to that of a hundred thousand moons. They fill my body and pacify all illnesses, evil spirits, negative karmic forces, mental obscurations and interferences to life. The lights then leaves via my pores and form a white circular halo around me approximately a span in depth. All activities of pacification are accomplished.

Again lights stream forth from the letters at my heart. Yellow in color, they fill my body and increase my lifespan, merits, qualities of learning and understanding, wisdoms of hearing, contemplation and meditation, and so forth. They leave my body and form a thin halo outside the white one previously constructed. All activities of increase are accomplished.

Lights once more radiate from the letters at my heart. Red in color, they grant me power over the three worlds. They leave my body and form a red halo outside the yellow one. Countless activities of power are accomplished.

Blue lines shine forth from the letters at my heart. They bestow upon me power to accomplish all activities. They leave my body and form a blue halo outside the red. All activities of destruction are accomplished.

Again lights proceed from the letters at my heart. Green in color, they bestow upon me attainments both common and supreme. They leave my body and come to form a green halo outside the blue one. All activities are accomplished.

Now brown lights shine forth from the letters at my heart and fill my body. All attainments are made firm. The lights leave my body and form a brown halo outside the green. All siddhis and blessings are made firm.

All six halos are oval-shaped, somewhat like eggs. They are so strong that even the wind that destroys an aeon could not move them. The spaces between them are so thickly filled with blue utpala flowers that nowhere is there an opening. Thus is great protection established.

White lights and a stream of nectars proceed from the mantra malas and fill my body. Illnesses, evil spirits, negative karmic forces, mental obscurations and obstacles to my life are quelled, and I attain the siddhi of immortality.

(Then, avoiding mistakes such as unclear mantra recitation and mental wandering, recite the mantras. Here there are two mantras to be applied: the mantra of increase and the essence mantra. According to the writings of Je Gendun Gyatso, the Second Dalai Lama, one should recite the former of these only a few hundred times at the beginning and end of each session, dedicating the main part of the sitting to the latter.)

(The Mantra of Increase:)

OṂ TĀRE TUTTĀRE TURE MAMA ĀYUḤ PUṆYE
JÑĀNA PUṢHṬHIṂ KURU SVĀHĀ.

(The Essence Mantra:)

OṂ TĀRE TUTTĀRE SVĀHĀ.

(When the prescribed number of the above mantras has been performed, recite the hundred syllable Padmasattva mantra to purify yourself of errors and to make firm the transforming powers attained. Then make the offerings and praise as before.

(Thirdly is the conclusion. This begins with the offering of the ritual cake:)

OṂ SVABHĀVA SHUDDAḤ SARVA DHARMĀḤ
SVABHĀVA SḤUDDHO HAṂ.

Everything becomes empty. From the sphere of emptiness appears the container of the ritual cake, a white letter TAṂ above it. TAṂ emits lights. They strike the container and transform it into a huge, vast, jewelled container. They strike the ritual cake and transforms it into an immense ocean of wisdom nectars.

OṂ ĀḤ HŪṂ (3X)
OṂ SVABHĀVA SHHUDDAḤ SARVA DHARMĀḤ
SVABĀVA SHUDDHO HAṂ!

Everything becomes empty. From the sphere of emptiness the PAṂ appears in the sky before me. PAṂ transforms into a lotus bearing a letter A. A transforms into a moon disk, at the center of which is a white letter TAṂ. TAṂ emits lights which make offerings to the High Ones, work the good of sentient beings and then recollect. The letter TAṂ transforms completely and white Tara, the Wish-Fulfilling Wheel, emerges. Her body is white in color, she has one face and two arms, seems as though sixteen years of age and is extremely beautiful. Her right hand is in the mudra Supreme Generosity and the thumb and ring finger of her left hand, which is poised at her heart, hold the stem of a white lotus. To symbolize the Buddhas of the three times, the lotus, spreads into three branches beside her ear: the middle branch bears a flower in full bloom; the right, one that has gone to fruit; and the left, an unopened bud. Her hair is tied up in a knot, she is adorned with the various ornaments and is clothed in silken-garments, Her back rests erect upon a moon disk, her entire body is of the nature of light and her feet are in the vajra-posture. White OṂ marks the crown of her head: red ĀḤ, her throat; and blue HŪṂ, her heart. As well, a white letter TAṂ rests upon a moon disk at her heart.

TAṂ emits beams of light, inviting exalted Tara, who is surrounded by masses of Buddhas and Bodhisattvas from her natural abode; JAḤ HŪṂ BAṂ HOḤ: they merge to become non-dual.

Again lights proceed from the seed letter TAṂ, inviting the Empowering Deities. They hold up vases filled with nectars of wisdom: OṂ SARVA TATHĀGATA ABHIṢHEKATA SAMAYA SHRĪYE ĀḤ HŪṂ.

Saying this, they initiate her with their ambrosial waters. Her body becomes filled with ambrosia and the surplus that overflows the crown of her head transforms into Amitabha who becomes her crown ornament.

(Making offerings to the deity in front:)

> OṂ SVABHĀVA SHUDDAḤ SARVA DHARMĀḤ SHUDDHO HĀṂ!

Everything becomes (seen as) emptiness. From the sphere of emptiness appear eight letters OṂ, which transform into huge, vast jewelled containers, inside each of which is an OṂ. The letters OṂ melt into light and reappear in the form of the offering substances:

water for the mouth, water for the feet, flowers, incense, light, scented oil, food and music. These are all pure and equal to the limits of the sky. OṂ ARGHAṂ ĀḤ HŪṂ, (and so forth, until SHABDE to consecrate them. Then:) OṂ ĀRYĀ TĀRE SAPARIVĀRA (and so forth, until SHABDE) PRATĪCHCHHA HŪṂ SVĀHĀ.

TĀRE, freedom from samsara;
TUTTĀRE, freedom from the eight terrors,
TURE, freedom from all illness:
Homage to Mother Tara.

(Making offerings to the deity in front:)

OM SVABHĀVA SHUDDAḤ SARVA DHARMĀḤ
SVABHĀVA SHUDDHO HĀṂ!

Everything becomes (seen as) emptiness. From the sphere of emptiness appear eight letters OṂ, which transform into huge, vast jewelled containers, inside each of which is an OṂ. The letters OṂ melt into light and reappear in the form of offering substances: water for the mouth, water for the feet, flowers, incense, light, scented oil, food and music. These are all pure and equal to the limits of the sky.

OṂ ARGHAṂ ĀḤ HŪṂ, (and so forth, until SHABDE to consecrate them. Then:)
OṂ ĀRYĀ TĀRE SAPARIVĀRA ARGHAṂ (and so forth, until SHABDE) PRATĪCHCHHA HŪṂ SVĀHĀ.

TĀRE, freedom from samsara;
TUTTĀRE, freedom from the eight terrors;
TURE, freedom from all illness;
Homage to Mother Tara.

Lights from the letter TAṂ at my heart shine forth and strike against all living beings, purifying them of negative karmic tendencies and mental obscurations. The beings transform into the exalted Tara and come before me. The Tara of the mandala before me and all beings in the form of Tara send out a tube of light from their tongues, by which the essence of the ritual cake is ingested and enjoyed.

OṂ ĀRYĀ TĀRE SAPARIVĀRA IDAṂ BALIṂTA KHA
KHA KHĀHI KHĀHI (7 or 21X)

(This method of offering the ritual cake to Tara and also to all beings as Tara is taken from the White Tara sadhana of Je Gendun Drub, the First Dalai Lama, and therefore is reliable.

Now make offerings and praises as before and offer prayers that your wishes and aims may be fulfilled. Then:)

Anything I have done incorrectly due to ignorance or lack of materials, with all mistakes in this ritual, O Tara, I beg you to forbear.

(Thus you should purify yourself of meditational mistakes and also should dedicate merits and recite verses of auspiciousness. Then, if you had arranged a consecrated image of Tara on your altar:)

O you who for the sake of living beings
Dwell within this image before me,
Bestow upon me health, life, prosperity
And the supreme siddhi of realizations.

(If you don't have one:)

VAJRA MUH: The Wisdom Beings return to their natural abodes. The Commitment Beings dissolve into me. The Wisdom Being aspect of the visualization of myself as Tara—VAJRA MUH—returns to its natural abode. The Commitment Being aspect of my mandala, beginning from the outside and working in, dissolves into light and then into me. I also dissolve, from feet up and head down, into light. This is absorbed into the letter TAṂ at my heart. TAṂ also gradually dissolves and disappears into clear light, like a rainbow into the sky.

(Rest there for a few moments. Then:) From the sphere of emptiness I instantly appear in the form of the exalted White Tara.

By the meritorious energy of this practice,
May I quickly attain the siddhi of Tara.
And may living beings without exception,
Be then led to that very state.

(Between meditation sessions, see all manifest forms as the body of Tara, understand all sounds as her voice and do not stray form the divine pride of seeing yourself as Tara. However, even though you see both yourself and others as the enlightened being Tara, maintain an awareness that all things have no inherent existence and have Thatness or emptiness, as their nature. Do not be distracted from this yogic training of the illusory nature of appearances.

When in retreat you should practice this meditation in either three or four sessions daily and persevere until you have collected three hundred thousand mantras. This is the method taught by many renowned sages of the past. Otherwise, continue the retreat until you see the form and hear the voice of Tara, or gain special realization, or until you receive special signs of having overcome death, such as dreaming of making small, White Tara statues, etc.

If you are doing the practice to benefit someone else, visualize that he/she is sitting before you on a moon disc amidst a halo of light. Lights stream forth from the letters at your heart, leave your body via your right nostril and enter the left nostril of the recipient. They fill his/her body completely and remove all obstacles to his/her life. Meditating in this manner, recite the mantra: OṂ TĀRE TUTTĀRE TURE *Name* ĀYUṆ PUṆYE JÑANĀ PUSHTHIṂ KURU SVĀHĀ.

The benefits of this practice are innumerable. To quote the great Atisha: "None of the worldly gods, such as Brahma, Vishnu, Shiva, and so forth, will be able to affect you. You will be able to crush the Lord of Death. Ill fortune and poverty will be eradicated. All misery, and even the eight great terrors, will be cleared away. You will gain the ordinary magical powers, will become excellent in expression and composition, and will become of sharp mind. In fact you will become a perfect Buddha. What need to say more?"

These are the general blessings of the practice of White Tara, the Wish-Fulfilling Wheel. Furthermore, in particular, untimely and premature death will be avoided, your wisdoms of learning and insight will increase and, ultimately, Buddhahood will be quickly attained.)

The colophon: This sadhana focussing upon white Tara, the Wish-Fulfilling Wheel was written by Gyalwa Kalzang Gyatso, the Seventh Dalai Lama, who claims to be inferior in tantric learning and experience, and also to lack all literary skills. Written at the request of Jigme Tanpai Gyatso of Do Kham, East Tibet, it takes as its basis the White Tara sadhana of the Laughing Melodious Gyalwa Gendun Gyatso, the Second Dalai Lama, but adds certain practices from the White Tara sadhanas of both Je Gendun Drub, the First Dalai Lama, and the omniscient Gyalwa Lozang Gyatso, the Fifth Dalai Lama. By any merits of my having written this sadhana focusing upon she, the mere sound of whose name dispels death, sickness and misery, and bestows long life, may the drum announcing victory over the four maras resound. May living beings find the city of the liberation of great enlightenment, and may all be cared for by Arya Tara eternally.

Translated by Glenn H. Mullin with Chomdze Tashi Wangyal.

A Sadhana Focusing Upon Green Tara

(Quickly Evoking Awakened Activity)

by

The First Dalai Lama (1391-1474)

(Aspirants who wish to practice meditation upon Arya Tara should arrange an altar and seat and, sitting in the vajra posture, begin the session by taking refuge and generating the bodhi-mind. Then the Svabhava mantra:)

OṂ SVABHĀVA SHUDDHOḤ SARVA DHARMĀḤ SVABHĀVA SHODDHO 'HAṂ.

Everything is emptiness. From within the sphere of emptiness in the space before me appears the syllable PAṂ. PAṂ transforms into a lotus marked by the syllable ĀḤ. ĀḤ transforms into a moon disc bearing the syllable TAṂ. TAṂ transforms into an utpala lotus marked by the syllable TAṂ, green in color.

Lights go out from this TAṂ, make offerings to the High Ones, fulfill the needs of all beings and then re-collects back together. There is a complete transformation and the exalted Arya Tara spontaneously appears, her body bluish green in color with one face and two hands. Her right hand is in the mudra of supreme generosity, and her left, at her heart, holds the stem of an utpala flower between thumb and forefinger, the blossom of which blooms beside her ear. Sitting with her right foot drawn in and left extended. She is beautifully arrayed with precious ornaments, a crown, tiara, earrings, necklaces, bracelets, arm-rings, anklets and so forth. Her shoulders are adorned by exquisite silks and her lower body covered by a celestial skirt. Her appearance is that of a sixteen year old girl gazing upon me with a smile of delight. The letter OṂ marks her crown, ĀḤ her throat and HŪṂ her heart.

Lights go out from the HŪṂ at her heart and invite the Exalted Arya Tara from the Potala Pure Land, surrounded by a multitude of Buddhas and Bodhisattvas.

From the supreme sphere of the Potala,
Born from the green syllable TAṂ,
The syllable TAṂ emitting
A radiance able to liberate beings;
Tara and retinue, I request you to come.
ĀRYĀ TĀRE.

JAḤ HŪṂ BAM HOḤ. They merge and become non-dual. Again lights go out from the HŪṂ at her heart, summoning the five families of Empowering Deities with their retinues.

"Pray, O Tathagatas, perform the empowerment."

They come forth holding up the vases filled with the nectars of initiation: OṂ SARVA TATHĀGATA ABHIṢHEKATA SAMAYA SHRĪYE HŪṂ.

The initiating waters flow to the crown of her head, entering her body and completely filling it, thus purifying all stains. The excess nectars swirl upwards from the ushnisha and transform into Amitabha, who becomes her crown ornament.

(One then cleanses and purifies the offerings:)

OṂ SARVA TATHĀGATA ĀRYĀ TĀRĀ SAPARIVĀRA ARGHAṂ PRATĪCHCHHA HŪṂ SVĀHĀ (and so forth, until SHABDE).

Homage to Arya Tara, at whose lotus feet
The gods and demigods bow their crowns.
Tara, mother of all Buddhas: to she
Who frees from all poverty I bow down.

(Then, the visualization for the mantra recitation:)

Upon a moon disc at her heart is the green syllable TAṂ, surrounded by the mantra OṂ TĀRE TUTTĀRE TURE SVĀHĀ. Lights emanate from this and perform the desired functions. Meditating in this way, the mantra is recited.

(The mantra given above is the Essence Mantra and is the mantra generally recited. There are several variants of the mantra to accomplish the various activities. Two important types of variants are known as "the formulas of increase" and "the formula of pacification." Some common usages of these variations are as follows.)

(To increase lifespan:)

OṂ TĀRE TUTTĀRE TURE MAMA ĀYUḤ PUSHṬHIM KURU SVĀHĀ.

(To increase meritorious energy:)

OṂ TĀRE TUTTĀRE TURE PUṆYA PUṢṬHIM KURU SVĀHĀ.

(To increase wisdom:)

OṂ TĀRE TUTTĀRE TURE PRAJÑĀ PUSHṬHIM KURU SVĀHĀ.

(To increase wisdom:)

OṂ TĀRE TUTTĀRE TURE KĪRTI PUṢHṬHIM KURU SVĀHĀ.

(To pacify illness and contagious diseases:)

OṂ TĀRE TUTTĀRE TURE SARVA JĀRA BHYAḤ SHĀNTI KURU SVĀHĀ.

(To pacify obstructions and hindrances:)

OṂ TĀRE TUTTĀRE TURE SARVA VIGHNA SHĀNTI KURU SVĀHĀ.

(To free the mind from distraction:)

OṂ TĀRE TUTTĀRE SARVA VIKULE BHYAḤ SHĀNTI KURU SVĀHĀ.

(To pacify disturbing dreams and nightmares:)

OṂ TĀRE TUTTĀRE TURE SARVA DURSO VADURMINI SHĀNTI KURU SVĀHĀ.

(Here the mantra is recited while holding the visualization that the mantra being used surrounds the TAṂ at her heart, sending out vast waves of light to accomplish the purposes.)

At the conclusion of the recitation, make offerings and praises as before. Conclude the session with any prayers and auspicious wishes that seem appropriate. Thereafter the Venerable Tara dissolves into the letter TAṂ, which dissolves into light and come to the crown of my head, coming to my heart via my Brahma aperture, becoming of one nature with my own mind.

The colophon: The above sadhana of Green Tara was written by Gendun Drub at the request of numerous spiritual friends when Gendun Drub was residing at the Ganden Monastery.

Translated by Graham Coleman with Glenn H. Mullin.

CHAPTER SIX
Miscellaneous Deities

A Method of Accomplishing White Achala

by

The Second Dalai Lama (1617-1682)

I bow down to my Master (one with) this excellent deity.

(With the aspiration to actualize the perfected white Immutable One, firstly meditate on taking refuge and generating an altruistic mind:)

I take refuge in the Buddha, I take refuge in the Teachings and
I take refuge in the Supreme Community until I gain enlightenment.
By the virtue I gather from practicing giving and the other perfections, may I attain Buddhahood in order to benefit all sentient beings.

(Contemplating the four immeasurables:)

May all beings be endowed with happiness.
May all beings be free of suffering.
May all beings never be separated from happiness
May all beings abide in equanimity undisturbed by the eight worldly attitudes of dualistic preconceptions.

(The mantra to correct mental perception:)

OṂ SVABHĀVA SHUDDHAḤ SARVA DHARMĀḤ SVABHĀVA SHUDDOḤ 'HAM

By nature everything is emptiness. Within the sphere of emptiness appears Pam which becomes an eight-petalled lotus. At its center is a Paṃ which becomes a sun-disc upon which is my own mind in the form of a white syllable Hūṃ. From it, rays of light pour forth to purify the negativities and obscurations of all sentient beings and to make offerings to the Buddhas and Bodhisattvas of the ten directions. Their wisdom, compassion, actions and extensive deeds condense into the rays which dissolve into the Hūm. It transforms, thus I emerge as the perfected Immutable One of glistening white hue like that of a snow mountain.

I have one face and two arms. My right hand brandishes a sword of wisdom in the space above me. At my heart my left hand, in the terrifying gesture, holds an adamantine noose. The sole of my right foot presses down on one sun cushion whilst my left knee rests on another. I have three round, bloodshot eyes and my mouth is gaping, the four fangs bared. My orange eyelashes and moustaches are curled upwards and my yellow-brown hair is bristling erect. I am adorned with a variety of precious ornaments and wear a silken skirt over the lower part of my body. White OṂ marks the crown of my head, red ĀḤ, my throat and blue HŪṂ, my heart.

HŪṂ emits rays which invite the wisdom Being, who resembles me, from his own abode, JĀḤ HŪṂ BAṂ HOḤ. We become one.

Once again rays go forth from the HŪṂ at my heart inviting the empowering deities. "Please will you all grant initiation to me here before you!" By dint of this request: OṂ VAJRA BHĀVA ABHIṢHIÑEHATU HŪṂ. They confer initiation with their nectar waters. The excess liquid that remains on the crown of my head as a protrusion transforms into an Akshobya adorning my head.

(Having contemplated thus, make offerings to clear interferences, purify and receive blessings:)

OṂ ĀRYA ACHALA SAPARIVĀRA ARGHAṂ (and so forth, until SHABDE) PRATHĪCHCHHA HŪṂ SVĀHĀ.

(A praise:)

I make obeisance to the protector, the fully enlightened Immutable One
You are the embodiment of all the Conquerors of the three times,
Your wrathful form is white resplendence like that of a snow-clad mountain
By mere recollection of you, the most excellent wisdom you bestow.

(The mantra recitation:)

At my heart is a moon disc upon which is my own mind in the form of a white syllable Hūṃ. Encircling it at the disc's periphery is the rosary-like ten syllable mantra OṂ CHAṆḌA MAHĀROṢHAṆA HŪṂ PHAṬ in block capital letters. They are white in color, edged with a tinge of red. An infinite amount of light comes forth form them filling the whole of my body, dispelling all the nescient darkness of my body, speech and mind. The light rays leave my body through the hair pores becoming offerings to the Buddhas and Bodhisattvas of the ten directions. Their compre-hension of wisdom as well as the three wisdoms of exposition, dialectics and composition of the wise and learned, the wisdom of those such as Brahma and Indra together with all such capabilities and strength, in short, all mundane and transcendent wisdom, gathers (into the rays) and absorbs into the HŪṂ at my heart.

(Recite the mantra silently while envisioning carefully wisdom's unimpeded illumination regarding exposition, dialectics and composition. When you have carried out the practice in this way, you may take as signs of accomplishment the appearance in dreams of the following: finding weapons like swords used as ritual hand implements, the rising of the sun or moon, blowing horns, hoisting victory banners or flags, wearing pure white clothing or climbing to the summit of high snow mountains.

If desired, end the session by offering a ritual cake thus: (arrange) a white ritual cake. Sprinkle a little of the inner offering. (Transform the cake) into nectar and bless it by (the incantation of) (OṂ ĀḤ HŪṂ.)

Rays of light from the seed syllable at my heart, invite to the space before me the fully enlightened Immutable One who resembles my own visualized form. The HŪM on his tongue becomes a single-spoked vajra (through which he imbibes the nectar's essence) by means of a hollow beam of light.

(Contemplate thus and offer three or seven recitations of:)

OṂ CHAṆḌA MAHĀ ROṢHAṆA HŪṂ PHAṬ BALIṂTA KHA KHA KHĀHI KHĀHI.

(A praise:)

I make obeisance to the protector, the fully enlightened Immutable One

You are the embodiment of all the Conquerors of the three times,
Your wrathful form is white resplendence like that of a snow-clad mountain
By mere recollection of you, the most excellent wisdom you bestow.

(Entreaties for fulfillment of one's wish (to improve wisdom:)

By properly constructing the vessel of hearing, contemplation and meditation
Fixing the vast sail of the perfect exalted attitude,
Driven by the wind of unrelenting perseverance,
May I free sentient beings from the ocean of cyclic existence.

However much I may have heard or have practiced great generosity
And whatever pure morality and discriminating wisdom I may possess,
Henceforth in my continuum, may these be surpassed
By my degree of freedom from all pride.

May I hear endless discourses without ever being satisfied
At the feet of a sage who has no need
To rely on other than the force of pure logic
For elucidating the precise meaning of the teachings.

By precise and correct analysis both day and night
Using the four types of reasoning regarding the meaning of what I have heard,
May I eradicate doubt by means of discerning introspection
Gained from contemplation of the substance of the doctrine.

When this is done and my contemplations have yielded conviction
Regarding the mode of existence of the extremely profound,
In solitude may I achieve correct (realization)
Through enthusiastic perseverance cutting attachment to this life.

By hearing, contemplating and meditating in this way
When the essence of the Buddha's thought develops in my continuum,
May there never arise notions of working for personal
Happiness or worldly conceptions clinging to the cyclic round.

May I enjoy repletion both spiritual and otherwise
Never parted from my Perfect Master in all lifetimes.
By comprehensively amassing the qualities of the paths and levels,
May I attain speedily the state of the Vajra Holder.

The colophon: This abbreviated method of accomplishing the white Immutable One was composed by the Buddhist monk Gendun Gyatso at Namsay Lhatse.

Translated into English with Chomdze Tashi Wangyal and Denma Locho Rinpoche.

A Sadhana Focusing on the Bodhisattva Maitreya

(A Stairway Leading to Tushita)

by

The Fifth Dalai Lama (1617-1682)

NAMO AJITAṆĀTHĀYA

By the clear compassion of Maitreya,
May we reap the rich harvest of victory,
And cool the sufferings of karma and delusions.
O, Incomparable Lord Maitreya,
Fifth Buddha of this fortunate aeon,
Inspire myself and all sentient beings
With the touch of your long arm of compassion.

In the presence of the Master,
Whose eyes blaze with light,
I kneel down with hands joined, and request:
That the promise of the Seat,
Like a carving in hard stone,
May not perish,

And the fruit of reciting your mantra
May be experienced.

O Protector, you give liberation
From the world's boundless sufferings;
And I constantly take refuge in you,
My able Captain.

Here, in simple words, is a sadhana which focuses on the Bodhisattva Maitreya, who was prophesied to manifest Great Enlightenment at the Vajra Seat. It is based on a Maitreya sadhana called "A Source of Fearlessness", as found in the scholar-yogin Abhyakara Gupta's well documented "Ocean of Mandalas"—a collection of 242 sadhanas. It is designed for recitation.

The practice consists of three parts: the preliminaries, the actual practice and the conclusion.

(Firstly, take refuge in the Objects of Refuge, as follows:)

I take refuge in the Spiritual Master.
I take refuge in the Buddha.
I take refuge in the Buddha's Teaching, the Dharma.
I take refuge in the Supreme Community, the Sangha. (3X)

For the sake of myself and all other sentient beings, I will attain the supreme state of a perfect Buddha. For this purpose, I shall take up the practice of the profound meditation on Arya Maitreya.

(Say this three times to generate the bodhi-mind. Then visualize the merit-field:)

In one instant, I arise as the Venerable Maitreya. A bright syllable HŪṂ at my heart radiates light, inviting Venerable Maitreya, who bears Guru Vajrasattva on his head as his crown ornament. Maitreya is surrounded by infinite numbers of Buddhas and Bodhisattvas who have come from their natural abodes. Vajra samājaḥ.

(Then make these offerings:)

OṂ VAJRA PUSHPE ĀḤ HŪṂ
OṂ VAJRA DHUPE ĀḤ HŪṂ
OṂ VAJRA ĀLOKE ĀḤ HŪṂ
OṂ VAJRA GANDHE ĀḤ HŪṂ
OṂ VAJRA NAIVIDYA ĀḤ HŪṂ
OṂ VAJRA SHABDE ĀḤ HŪṂ

(Next make general confession and meditate on the Four Immeasurables as follows:)

I take refuge in the Three Jewels;
I confess each of my negative deeds;
I rejoice in the virtue of all beings;
I firmly resolve on Enlightenment;
I take refuge in Buddha, Dharma and the Supreme Community
Until I reach Enlightenment;
In order to benefit myself and others,
I generate the bodhi-mind.
Having developed the supreme bodhi-mind,
I will take care of all sentient beings as my guests;
I will follow the excellent ways of the Bodhisattvas;
For the sake of all beings, I will attain Enlightenment.
May all sentient beings come to possess happiness and its causes.
May all sentient beings become separated from suffering and its causes.
May all sentient beings never be separated from the happiness which is beyond suffering.
May all sentient beings come to possess a state of perfect equanimity, not feeling close to some and distant from others.

(Say this three times.)

(Secondly, meditate on the actual practice:)

OṂ SVABHĀVA SHUDDHAḤ SARVA DHARMĀḤ SVABHĀVA SHUDDHO 'HAṂ All becomes seen as empty (of self-existence).

In the sphere of emptiness, my own mind appears as a yellow syllable MAIṂ, from which light radiates. It pleases the Enlightened Ones by bringing them offerings. Then it purifies the negative karma and obscurations of all sentient beings. The light collects back into the MAIṂ, which transforms into the syllable PAṂ. This in turn transforms into a lotus marked by ĀḤ. This ĀḤ becomes a moon cushion, on top of which I arise as three-faced Ārya Maitreya. My main face is yellow, saffron-like in color. My right face is black, and my left, white. Each face has three eyes; each is peaceful and smiles. My dark hair is tied up in a knot. The first two of my four hands are at my heart, in the mudra expressing the turning of the Wheel of Dharma. My lower right hand is in the mudra of Supreme Generosity, and my lower left hand holds a fragrant dark-yellow flower. I am adorned by eight precious ornaments: head ornaments, earrings, a neckband, armbands, bracelets, anklets, shoulder-belts, and long crystal necklaces. Heavenly silks cover the upper half of my body, and I wear a panchalika skirt. A full moon is my backrest, for I am seated in the Sattvasana, in the center of a halo of light. My forehead is marked by the syllable OṂ, my throat by ĀḤ, my heart by HŪṂ. At my heart stands a yellow MAIṂ on a moon-disc. It radiates light, inviting the Wisdom Beings, who are similar to myself, from their actual abodes:

VAJRA SAMĀJAḤ
JAḤ HŪṂ BAṂ HOḤ
They merge and become non-dual with me.

Once more light radiates forth, inviting the Empowering Deities of the Five Families, together with their entourage:

VAJRA SAMĀJAḤ

"Please, Tathagatas, bestow upon me the actual empowerment." Having thus been requested, they bestow the initiation with water from their vases, saying:

OṂ SARVA TATHĀGATA ABHISHEKATA SAMAYA SHRĪYE HŪṂ

It fills my body, and cleanses me of all stains. The surplus water overflows, transforming into Vajrasattva, who becomes my crown ornament.

(Next make offerings of the five kinds of materials and music to the merit field:)

OṂ VAJRA PUṢHPE PRATĪCHCHHA HŪṂ SVĀHĀ
OṂ VAJRA DHUPE PRATĪCHCHHA HŪṂ SVĀHĀ
OṂ VAJRA ĀLOKE PRATĪCHCHHA HŪṂ SVĀHĀ
OṂ VAJRA GANDHE PRATĪCHCHHA HŪṂ SVĀHĀ
OṂ VAJRA NAIVIDYA PRATĪCHCHHA HŪṂ SVĀHĀ
OṂ VAJRA SHABDA PRATĪCHCHHA HŪṂ SVĀHĀ

The fire of Great Love burns the fuel of anger,
The light of wisdom clears the darkness of ignorance
I bow down to you, King of the Dharma
Abiding in Tushita, who protects all beings.

(Having completed this praise, then recite the following:)

Upon a moon mandala at my heart is a letter MAIṂ, encircled by the mantra OṂ MAITREYA SVĀHĀ. These letters radiate light, which makes offerings to the Enlightened Ones, and purify the negative karma and the obscurations of sentient beings, placing them in the supreme state of Arya Maitreya. The light collects and reabsorbs into the seed-syllable.

(Continue with this visualization while reciting this powerful mantra:)

OṂ MAITREYA SVĀHĀ

"O Tathagatas, please bless myself and all sentient beings to be able to accomplish the ordinary and supreme siddhis."

(Having made this request, make offerings and praises:)

OṂ VAJRA PUṢHPE PRATĪCHCHHA HŪṂ SVĀHĀ
OṂ VAJRA DHUPE PRATĪCHCHHA HŪṂ SVĀHĀ
OṂ VAJRA ĀLOKE PRATĪCHCHHA HŪṂ SVĀHĀ
OṂ VAJRA GANDHE PRATĪCHCHHA HŪṂ SVĀHĀ
OṂ VAJRA NAIVIDYA PRATĪCHCHHA HŪṂ SVĀHĀ
OṂ VAJRA SHABDE PRATĪCHCHHA HŪṂ SVĀHĀ

The fire of Great Love burns the fuel of anger,
The light of Wisdom clears the darkness of ignorance.
I bow down to you, King of the Dharma
Abiding in Tushita, who protects all beings.

(Next recite the hundred-syllable mantra three times:)

OṂ VAJRASATTVA SAMAYA, (etc)

Anything I have done incorrectly, due to not finding the
materials, due to lack of knowledge or my inability,
I beg you, Lord Maitreya, to forbear!

VAJRA MUḤ The Wisdom Beings return (to their abodes).

While I visualize myself as the Commitment Being, I have at my forehead the syllable OṂ, at my throat ĀḤ, at my heart HŪṂ.

(Now recite whatever prayers and verses of auspiciousness you wish, such as the following by the first Dalai Lama:)

May all beings, who create harmonious conditions
For the building of wondrous images of Maitreya,

Experience the glory of Dharma's Supreme Vehicle,
In the presence of the venerable protector, Maitreya.

When Lord Maitreya appears like a rising sun
Over the mountains around Bodhgaya,
May the lotus of my wisdom be opened
For the sake of the fortunate bee-like beings.

At that time will Victorious Maitreya
Smilingly place his right hand on my head,
And predict when and where I shall attain Enlightenment:
May I quickly gain Buddhahood for the sake of all.

In all my lifetimes, until my Enlightenment,
May I collect together, and practice to perfection,
All the vast and powerful ways
Of Buddhas and Bodhisattvas, past, present and future.

Holding the olden staff of wisdom, on which flies
The painted flag of excellent teachings
Adorned with a jewel of the Three Higher Trainings,
May I carry the victory banner of the Doctrine to the ten directions.

May all Doctrines, which are sources
Of goodness and happiness,
Be enriched and strengthened;
May all upholders of the Doctrine live in good health;
And may the Buddha's Doctrine flourish
As a source of happiness and joy for all.

By the power of meditating constantly on the three kinds of love,
May there be auspicious signs of Lord Maitreya,
Who crushes the maras with the force of love,
And protects all living beings by love's power.

Dedication:

Through the merit I gain by practicing this,
May all beings be freed from the bad circumstances
Of hell, and of being pretas, animals and asuras.

The colophon: This particular sadhana of Maitreya, "A Stairway Leading to Tushita", is a fuller version of the Maitreya sadhana found in the "Ocean of Mandalas" (Skt.: Vajravali Nama Mandala Sadhana) written by the tantricist Abhayakara Gupta. It was written, at the request of Namkha Wangpo and Rewa Losang Dorje, by the Omniscient Lord of Knowledge and Compassion, the Bande from Zahor (the Fifth Dalai Lama), with the help of the scribe and master of tantric dance—Gelong Ngawang Konchog.

Translated by the Buddhist monk Hans Van der Bogaert, with Gen Sonam Rinchen.

THE IMMUTABLE SARASVATI

(Expanding Wisdom's Illumination)

by

The Second Dalai Lama (1475-1542)

Exquisitely you came forth as the Swan Child, Sarasvati,
From the immaculate lotus mouth of the Perfected One.
I will explain the steps leading to your actualization,
And to the perpetual integration in the vastness of my mind.

(With the aspiration to actualize the goddess, White Sarasvati, begin with the general preliminaries. These commence with the taking of refuge and the generation of the altruistic mind of enlightenment. Then, visualize:)

Instantly, I arise as the goddess Sarasvati. At my heart is the syllable HRĪH, from which light radiates to invite the goddess Sarasvati, who is inseparable from my root Spiritual Master and who is accompanied by hosts of Buddhas and Bodhisattvas.

(Make offerings with great devotion, in order that they may remain here before you:)

OṂ SARASVATĪ ARGHAṂ (and so on until SHABDA)
PRATĪCHCHHA HŪṂ SVĀHĀ

(Then, take the pledges of the altruistic mind of enlightenment. And, to complete the general preliminaries for the accumulation of merit, contemplate the four immeasurables. Next, for the accumulation of insights, recite the following mantra, while pondering its meaning. Be aware that all phenomena within and beyond cyclic existence lack true existence: their intrinsic nature is identical with that of your mind:)

OṂ SHŪNYATĀ JÑĀNA VAJRA SVABHĀVA ĀTMA-KO 'HAṂ

By nature everything is emptiness. Within the sphere of emptiness appears the syllable PAṂ, which becomes an eight-petalled white lotus. At its center stands the syllable ĀḤ. This becomes a soothing white full moon-disc. Upon this disc is my mind—in the form of a white syllable HRĪḤ, from which light radiates. The light becomes offerings to all the Buddhas and Bodhisattvas; it also destroys the entire mental darkness enveloping all sentient beings, who thereby gain wisdom's illumination. The rays re-collect into the HRĪḤ. It transforms, and thus I emerge as the goddess Sarasvati, white in color. I have one face and two arms. My left hand holds a many-stringed vina—the type used by the celestial musicians. Its main hollow gourd resting by my left side. I pluck its strings with the plectrum-rings that adorn my right fingers. I sit with both legs crossed at the ankles and with both knees raised. I wear a mantle and skirt of various silks, and I am adorned with a precious diadem, a necklace, a longer hanging necklace, and an ornamented belt. Half of my sapphire-blue colored hair falls to my waist in tresses; the rest is braided and coiled at the crown of my head, and adorned with a flower garland. Above the garland is a flawless crown jewel and a crescent moon. The white syllable OM marks the crown of my head, a red ĀḤ my throat, and an indigo HŪṂ my heart. At my heart and standing upright is a white syllable AṂ, symbolizing essential life-giving forces.

While I exhale, hook-shaped lights come from the "M" of the "AṂ" and leave my body through the right nostril. They travel south, to the place known as the Pleasure Ground of Celestial Musicians situated on the shore of a vast ocean. The goddess Sarasvati resides there. The hook-shaped lights enter her left nostril and go to the wheel of wisdom at her heart. They attach themselves to the wheel in the way hooks are wont to do. The rays—now enhanced—leave from her right nostril and I invite them to return with the speed of a shooting star to the space before me.

(The invitation:)

OṂ PRITĪ DEVĪ HRĪḤ PUSHPE ĀḤ HŪṂ (and so on till SHABDA)

(Then:)

JAḤ HŪṂ BAṂ HOḤ

At the same time as I inhale, the hook-shaped lights enter my left nostril, but now in the form of circles of light. These then dissolve into the AṂ at my heart.

The AṂ transforms and there now appears at my heart the wheel of wisdom of Sarasvati. Upon this wheel is an eight-petalled white lotus. At the center of the lotus is a full moon-disc. My mind stands upon this disc in the form of an upright white syllable HRĪḤ. On each petal of the lotus are two syllables. They are all brilliantly white. Starting from the front petal, and going clockwise around the lotus they are: A Ā I Ī U Ū RI RĪ LI LĪ E AI O AU AṂ ĀḤ. Their light fills the whole of my body with clear radiance, just as the lamp's light pervades the area around it. This light clears away all my mental darkness, and I gain wisdom's pervasive illumination into all phenomena—particularly into the wisdoms concerning exposition, dialectics and composition.

(Meditate extensively on the great bliss that pervades your body, speech and mind. Having done so, proceed to recite HRĪḤ, and accompany this with the following contemplation. With each recitation, a circle of HRĪḤ syllables come forth, like licking flames, from the "H" of the HRĪḤ at your heart. The circles come out of your body through your mouth, and re-enter through your navel, dissolving back into the HRĪḤ at your heart. This wheel of light-rays revolves rapidly like a whirling firebrand, and with each recitation of HRĪḤ you destroy all your negativities and obscurations accumulated since beginningless time. In particular, you destroy all your mental darkness, and so continue to recite within that ambit of wisdom's illumination.

(Then, immeasurable rays of light go forth from the HRĪḤ at the center of the wheel at your heart, in order to gather—in the form of light—the knowledge and wisdom of all Buddhas, Bodhisattvas, Listeners, and Self-enlighteners; the three wisdoms of exposition, dialectics and composition of Brahma, Indra and all those who are wise and learned; the sun, moon, planets, and constellations; jewels; medicinal extracts and elixirs; the essence of all crops; and the longevity, merits, power and grandeur of all sentient beings. These dissolve into the HRĪḤ, and your whole body is flooded with radiance. At this point, contemplate that you have actualized every conceivable excellence within and beyond cyclic existence.

(The recitation of this syllable one hundred and twenty-five thousand times is said to be adequate, but only if unimpaired by interpolations or by excessively fast or slow recitation. It would be better to say the syllable half a million times, or until a sign of actualization is gained. During the recitation, include all sentient beings—not just yourself—in the contemplation. Carefully visualize them all as the goddess Sarasvati, each with their own wheel of wisdom. They are reciting the syllable, and all their defilements and obscurations are cleansed. Thus they gain wisdom's illumination. Your attainment will come rapidly when you practice this way.

(For the conclusion of the session, do the contemplation on the accumulation of all good qualities and excellences—especially the remarkable enormity of the wisdoms of exposition, dialectics and composition. This is done exactly as before, and makes use of the HRĪḤ at your heart. Then visualize the light completely flooding every particle of your body. This sense of the light being completely pervasive should be unshakable from moment to moment.

(End with some dedications of merit and some prayers, for example:)

By this virtue, may I quickly accomplish the powerful attainments of Sarasvati, and may I lead all sentient beings without exception to that state.

May I develop the precious awakening mind that is latent within me, and may that which I have go from strength to strength.

(Signs which may appear as a result of successful practice are, for example, an improved memory, the ability to recite mantras rapidly and clearly, an understanding into the import of many scriptural texts, and even a wish to write poetry. You may also have dreams of being offered curd, milk or butter by beguiling maidens wearing much jewelry; of eating or being given fruit or the best of medicines; of being offered chalk, rare and valuable wood, or jewel and flower garlands; of seeing the sun or moon rise; of picking flowers; or of constantly bathing in pure, clean water.

(If the practice has been done properly, yet none of the above signs have appeared, and the object of visualization lacks clarity, you should merge the "ĪḤ" of the HRĪḤ visualized at your heart into the "HR", which turns upside down and emerges from your body at the navel. You can then vary the visualization by meditating on the return of this letter through the mouth into the body, and its subsequent absorption—but now in the form of HRĪḤ—at the heart. Or You could single-pointedly practice absorption and meditation on the action of the sixteen syllables.

(A small amount of practice of any wrathful deity, such as Hayagriva, is advisable in order to ward off interferences which might greatly hinder your accomplishment in this practice; practices such as offering of ritual cakes to any of the wealth deities are also suggested to preclude the more mundane handicap of poverty.)

(How to offer a ritual cake in between sessions: place a ritual cake made with the three pure foods—curd, milk and butter—in a clean container. Sprinkle a little of the inner offering to clear interferences. Recite the following mantra to correct your mental perception:)

> OṂ SVABHĀVA SHUDDHAḤ SARVA DHARMĀḤ
> SVABHĀVA SHUDDHO 'HAṂ

(Transform the cake into an immense expanse of nectar, and bless this by reciting):

> OṂ ĀḤ HŪṂ (3X)

I invite into the space before me the goddess Sarasvati, who is identical in appearance with my own visualized form. From her tongue comes a hollow beam of light which enables her to imbibe the nectar's essence in its entirety.

> OṂ SARASVATĪ HRĪḤ AKAROMUKHAṂ SARVA
> DHARMĀNĀṂ ADHYANUTPAN NATVAD OṂ ĀḤ
> HŪṂ PHAṬ SVĀHĀ (5 or 7X)

(This mantra request her to partake of the offering. She does so, and is delighted by it. After this contemplation, make an outer offering:)

> OṂ SARASVATĪ ARGHAṂ (and so on till SHABDA)
> PRATĪHCCHHA HŪṂ SVĀHĀ

(Now follows as praise:)

> I make obeisance at your feet, O Sarasvati;
> Your body, bewitching and entrancing goddess,
> Was engendered from the immaculate speech of
> Avalokiteshvara,

Whose magical creations embody the wisdom of all the
Victorious Ones.

I bow down to you, most vibrant maid of sixteen,
Your body's beauty is as splendid as Mount Kailash,
Your face is one hundred times more exquisite than the
autumn moon,
And your entrancing eyes are as delightful as the sight
of a group of blue lotuses.

I bow down to you. Your cross-legged pose is elegant,
And with your two hands, you make the sweet harmonies
of the celestial musicians.
Your voice is a honey-sweet stream;
An abundant elixir for all who hear.

I bow down to you, Sarasvati, for you can bestow
Perfection in the skills of exposition, dialectics and
composition,
By means of the radiance of the syllable HRIḤ,
The circle of letters and the wheel of wisdom at the heart.

All the wise are delighted by skillful composition;
And the defeat of all opponents is the mark of an expert
debater.
Lucid expression thrills every sharp mind. So, please
Bestow on me the wisdoms of exposition, dialectics and
composition.

(Following these meaningful entreaties, visualize:)

As I breathe in, simultaneously, the goddess visualized before me dissolves into me. (Conclude with auspicious verses and dedications of merit, such as:) I dedicate these merits, as dauntless Manjushri and Samantabhadra did of yore. May I train and emulate their perfect realization.

May I enjoy contentment, both spiritual and otherwise,
And never be parted from my perfect Master in all
lifetimes.
By amassing the qualities of the paths and levels,
May I attain soon the state of the Vajra Holder.

The colophon: This graded method in the practice of Sarasvati, the goddess of eloquence, is called "Expanding Wisdom's Illumination".

It sets forth in its entirety the pith of my Master's wisdom and instruction, and was composed at the gracious insistence of Rinchen Kunga Chokyong Dragpa Namgyal, a great king of religion, a man of formidable and unsullied wisdom in all fields of learning. An upright monk, noble Gendun Gyatso, composed it in the Palace of Happiness (in Drepung Monastery). It was recorded by the author's scribe Kachupa Yonten.

Translated by Kevin Garratt with Chomdze Tashi Wangyal.

A Sitataptra Sadhana

by

The Seventh Dalai Lama (1708-1757)

O Bhagavati, you embrace all aspects of phenomena
With the expanse of the white parasol that is your stainless wisdom,
And you remove the tormenting diseases that are samsara and selfish peace.
Please remove all obstacles and confer the supreme and common siddhis.

This sadhana draws water from a river
That carries precious sands of siddhis:
The River Ganga, the god flowing from Mt Kailash,
Is condensed into the stage of this practice.

(There are many different traditions in the steps to the kriya tantra sadhana of Ushnisha Sitatapatra, who is of the Tathagata family. However, Chime Namka Drag of Nartang has made a compilation of a great many source materials, such as the sadhana tradition of the great and noble Atisha. The following is the sadhana and practice of Sitatapatra with three faces and six hands which is drawn from this famous "One Hundred Root Texts of Nartang":)

I take refuge in the Buddha, Dharma,
And the Supreme Assembly until enlightenment.
By the merit from my actions such as generosity
May I accomplish Buddhahood to help all sentient beings.
May all sentient beings have happiness.
May all sentient beings be free from suffering.
May all sentient beings never be without happiness.

May all sentient beings remain in equanimity, unmoved by the eight worldly concerns or by preconceptions about an object apprehended and the mind which apprehends it.

(After you have taken refuge and generated the bodhi-mind as well as the four immeasurables (as above), making sure that the meaning has suffused your mental stream, not just the words, visualize the following:)

In an instant, with clarity I arise as Ushnisha Sitatapatra. Light radiates from the seed syllable at my heart. It invites Sitatapatra and all her surrounding host of Buddhas and Bodhisattvas from their natural abodes and they take their places in space before me.

(Make offerings:)

OṂ VAJRA ARGHAṂ (and so on until SHABDA) ĀḤ HŪṂ

(If you are doing this more elaborately, make the seven-limb prayer according to any well-known version:)

(Then visualize:)

The figures of the merit fields depart to their natural abodes.

(And then:)

OṂ SVABHĀVA SHUDDHAḤ SARVA DHARMĀḤ SVABHĀVĀ SHUDDHO 'HAM

Everything transforms into emptiness.

Within the state of emptiness, from a PAṂ, a lotus arises and from an A, a moon mandala. On top of this is my own mind, in the form of a white seed syllable OṂ. Light radiates from this and carries out the two purposes (my own and that of other sentient beings). This reabsorbs and transforms into myself as Arya Sitatapatra. My main face is white, the right one is blue and the left one red. Each of the three faces has three eyes. My six hands hold the following: the right three hold a wheel, an arrow and a hook (respectively); the left three hold the wrathful mudra, a bow and a sword. My hair is tied up in a top-knot and I am wearing precious ornaments and silken raiment. I sit with my feet in the Bodhisattva position in the midst of a concentration of transparent light. On the top of my head is a white OṂ, at my throat a red ĀḤ and at the heart a blue HŪṂ. My heart is also marked by the white seed syllable OṂ. Light radiates from this which invites the wisdom beings from their natural abodes. They are just like the form I am meditating on.

> OṂ ARGHAṂ (and so on until SHABDA) PRATĪCH-CHHAYE SVĀHĀ
>
> JAḤ HŪṂ BAṂ HOḤ

They become inseparable.

Then light radiates from the HŪṂ at my heart and invites the initiation deities. I beseech them, "All of you Tathagatas, please confer true initiation on me." Holding vases full of nectars of transcendental wisdom, they reply,

> "OṂ SARVA TATHĀGATA ABHISHEKATA SAMAYA SHRĪYE HŪṂ,"

and confer the initiation with the water in the vases. It fills my whole body dispelling all stains. The excess water overflows at the crown of my head and transforms into Vairochana adorning my head.

(The offerings:)

(Say the following while sending away hindrances:)

> OṂ ĀḤ VIGHNĀNATA SHRĪ HRA HŪṂ

(Purify everything into emptiness:)

> OṂ SVABHĀVA SHUDDHAḤ, SARVA DHARMĀḤ SVABHĀVA SHUDDHO 'HAṂ

Everything transforms into emptiness.

Within the state of emptiness, there arises an OṂ which becomes a great, enormous, precious container. Inside it an OṂ melts into light which produces water to drink, water for the feet, flowers, incense, lamps, perfume, food and music. These are transparent and rapidly multiply to become as extensive as space itself.

(Bless these offerings:)

> OṂ ARGHAṂ ĀḤ HŪṂ (and so on through to SHABDA).

(Offer these with:)

OṂ UṢHṆĪṢHA SITATĀPATRĀ ARGHAṂ (and so on until SHABDA) PRATĪCHCHHA HŪṂ SVĀHĀ

You were born from the compassionate Sugata's ushnisha,
You annihilate those who would harm this doctrine, the source of bliss,
And you confer the results of health and happiness.
I prostrate and praise you, Bearer of the White Parasol of supreme bliss.

At my heart is a moon mandala. On top of it is the seed syllable OṂ surrounded by the recitation mantra. Light radiates from these and purifies all sickness, evil spirits and hindrances. And I obtain all the siddhis of the body, speech and mind of the Bhagavati.

(Recite the following as many times as you can, not letting the mind distract to other thoughts away from anything to be found in contemplations such as the one just above:)

TADYATĀ, OṂANALE ANALE, PIṢHADE PIṢHADE PIṢHADE, VAIRA VAIRA, VAJRADHARĪ, BANDA BANDUNĪ HŪṂ PHAṬ SVĀHĀ

(Visualize:)

The wisdom beings (invoked during) the generation of myself as the deity separate from me and take their places in space before me.

(Make offering and praise just as before:)

OṂ UṢHṆĪṢHA SITĀTAPATRĀ ARGHAṂ (and so on till SHABDA) PRATĪCHCHHA HŪṂ SVĀHĀ

You were born from the compassionate Sugata's ushnisha,
You annihilate those who would harm this doctrine, the source of bliss,
And you confer the results of health and happiness.
I prostrate to you and praise you, Bearer of the White Parasol of supreme bliss.

(Beseech them to give all that you desire with the following and similar requests:)

Bhagavati Sitatapatra, please completely pacify all the sickness, evil spirits and hindrances of all sentient beings and please confer every single siddhi.

(Then recite the hundred-syllable mantra:)

OṂ PADMA SATTVA SAMAYA, MANU PĀLAYA, PADMA SATTVA TVENO PATISHṬHA, DṚIḌHO ME BHĀVA, SUTOṢHYO ME BHĀVA, SUPOṢHYO ME BHĀVA, ANURAKTO ME BHĀVA, SARVA SIDDHIM ME PRAYACHCHHA, SARVA KARMA SUCHA ME, CHITTAṂ SHRĪYAṂ KURU HŪṂ, HA HA HA HA HOḤ BHAGAVĀN, SARVA TATHĀGATA, PADMA MA ME MUÑCHA, PADMA BHĀVĀ, MAHĀ SAMAYA SATTVA ĀḤ HŪṂ PHAṬ

(To beg forgiveness, recite the following, etc.:)

Please, O Protectors, be patient
With all that I have done and would have done,
But either did not carry out or in doing so, lapsed in concentration
Because of mental blindness.

(Visualize:)

The wisdom beings depart to their natural abodes and gradually the commitment being becomes unfocused emptiness.

(Then make prayer, dedicate (the merit) and extent the unfocused emptiness further:)

By this merit, when I have accomplished
The state of Ushnisha Sitatapatra,
May I lead every single
Sentient being to that state.

The colophon: The above sadhana of Bhagavati Sitatapatra was requested by Bhikshu Losang Gyaltsen (Known in Mongolian as) Gunsai Ne-er Getaichen of the Neirin Tribe. He mentioned that an easy sadhana was needed and thus the Buddhist Bhikshu Losang Kalsang Gyatso composed it. It was dictated to the Abbot and Chief Celebrant of the Monastery.

Translated by Michael Richards, with Yeshe Lodoe Rinpoche.

A Vajra Vidarana Sadhana

by

The Fifth Dalai Lama (1617-1682)

Great hero, you conquer hordes of hindrances
By the force of your almighty, blazing vajra-power.
Supreme deity, as you stand firmly at the center of the lotus at my heart
I will briefly write your sadhana and daily practice.

(What to meditate on and recite in the daily practice of Vajra Vidarana follows.

(Take refuge and generate the bodhi-mind by repeating three times:)

I take refuge in the Buddha, Dharma
And the Supreme Assembly until enlightenment.
By the merit from my actions such as generosity,
May I accomplish Buddhahood to help all sentient beings.

(The merit field:)

Within my heart on a lotus and sun disc, a blue-green HŪṂ arises. From it light radiates, filling my body, purifying my sins and obscurations, and spreading out from my crown aperture. The light rays invite Vajra Vidarana and the Buddhas and Bodhisattvas surrounding him from their natural abodes.

VAJRA SAMĀJAḤ

(In obeisance say:)

NAMOḤ SARVA TATHĀGATA VAJRA VIDĀRAṆA SAPARIVĀRE BHYAḤ

(Make offering with:)

OṂ SARVA TATHĀGATA VAJRA VIDĀRAṆA SAPARIVĀRE ARGHAṂ (and so on until SHABDA) PRATĪCHCHHAYE SVĀHĀ

(Recite the following:)

I take refuge in the Three Jewels

I confess each and every sin.
I rejoice in the merit of all beings.
I set my heart on the enlightenment of a Buddha.

I take refuge until enlightenment
In the Buddha, Dharma and Supreme Assembly.
I will generate the bodhi-mind
So that I completely realize the purposes of myself and others.

Having developed this supreme bodhi-mind
I shall care for all beings as my guests and
I shall delight in supreme, enlightened deeds.
May I accomplish Buddhahood to benefit all beings!

May all sentient beings have happiness.
May all sentient beings be free from suffering
May all sentient beings never be without happiness.

May all sentient beings remain in equanimity, unmoved by the eight worldly concerns or by preconceptions about an object apprehended and the mind which apprehends it.

(The actual practice:)

OṂ SVABHĀVA SHUDDHAḤ SARVA DHARMĀḤ
SVABHĀVA SHUDDHO HAṂ

Everything transforms into emptiness.

Within the state of emptiness, from a PAṂ, a lotus arises, and from a RAṂ, a sun mandala. On it there is a HŪṂ which becomes a multi-colored vajra-cross marked by a HŪṂ. From this light radiates forming a vajra tent, a celestial palace and a wall of flame. Within all these, from PAṂ, a lotus arises and, from RAṂ, a sun disc. On it is a HŪṂ which becomes a multicolored vajra-cross marked by a HŪṂ. Light radiates from this which carries out the two purposes (my own and that of other sentient beings). The light reabsorbs and the vajra-cross transforms into myself as Vajra Vidarana, whose body is blue-green. I have one face, two hands and three eyes. My right hand holds to my heart a multicolored vajra-cross, and my left, at my hip, a bell with a vajra-cross handle. Although my face is somewhat wrinkled from which I am smiling a little I am distinguished by silken raiment and precious ornaments. My feet are in the vajra posture. At my forehead is an OṂ, at my throat an ĀḤ and at my heart a HŪṂ. Light radiates from the HŪṂ and invites wisdom beings who are just like the form on which I am meditating.

VAJRA SAMĀJAḤ

(Make offerings to them as before:)

NAMOḤ SARVA TATHĀGATA VAJRA VIDĀRAṆA SAPARIVĀRE BHYAḤ
OṂ SARVA TATHĀGATA VAJRA VIDĀRANA SAPARIVĀRE ARGHAṂ (and so on till SHABDA) PRATICHCHHAYE SVĀHĀ

(They dissolve into you:)

JAḤ HŪṂ BAṂ HOḤ

Again light radiates and invites the five classes of Buddhas and their retinues.

(Make offering to them:)

PAÑJAKŪLA SAPARIVĀRA ARGHAṂ (and so on until SHABDA) PRATĪCHCHAYE SVĀHĀ

(Pray and entreat them:)
O Tathagatas! Please confer true initiation on me.

OṂ SARVA TATHĀGATA ABHISHEKATA SAMAYA SHRĪYE HŪṂ

Saying this, they confer the initiation.

My body fills (with water) purifying my stains. The excess liquid overflows on top and becomes Vajrasattva adorning my head.

(Make offering to him as before:)

OṂ VAJRASATTVA SAPARIVĀRA ARGHAṂ (and so on until SHABDA) PRATĪCHCHHAYE SVĀHĀ

(The praise:)

I prostrate to Vajra Vidarana;
You utterly defeat the powers of the four Maras
By the power of every precious, fiery vajra,
Because your mind is the wisdom of non-duality.

(Recite this mantra while visualizing the multicolored vajra-cross surrounded by the mantra at your heart:)

NAMOSH CHAṆḌAPA VAJRA KRODHĀYA, HULU HULU, RIṢHṬHA RIṢHṬHA, BANDHA BANDHA, HANA HANA, AMṚITE HŪṂ PHAṬ

The wisdom beings (who were invited during) the generation of myself (as the deity) go before me in space.

(Make offering and praise to them:)

OṂ SARVA TATHĀGATA VAJRA VIDĀRAṆA SAPARIVĀRA ARGHAṂ (and so on till SHABDA) PRATĪCHCHHAYE SVĀHĀ

I prostrate to Vajra Virandana;
You utterly defeat the powers of the four Maras
By the power of every precious, fiery vajra,
Because your mind is the wisdom of non-duality.

(Then with this prayer beseech them:)

O Tathagatas! Please confer every siddhi without exception on all sentient beings and myself!

(Rectify any faults by:)

OṂ VAJRA SARVA HŪṂ

Please, O Protectors, be patient
With all that I have done and would have done,
But either did not carry out or lapsed in concentration
Because of my mental blindness.

(Visualize that the wisdom beings depart to their natural abodes when you snap your fingers and say:)

OṂ VAJRA MŪḤ

(Dedicate the virtue:)

By this merit, when I have accomplished
The state of Vajra Vidarana,
May I quickly lead every single
Sentient being to that state.

The colophon: Pilnag Ngondrub requested a very brief daily

practice of Vajra Vidarana and this Zahor monk (the Fifth Dalai Lama) composed it in accordance to his wishes.

Translated by Michael Richards, with Yeshe Lodoe Rinpoche.

A VAJRASATTVA GURU-YOGA METHOD

by

The Seventh Dalai Lama (1708-1757)

I make obeisance at the lotus feet of my Immaculate
  Master,
The inspiration of all wholesome and uplifting endeavor,
A true Bodhisattva guiding all sentient beings to
  happiness
In a state of complete and fearless emancipation.

(Herein is set out the Guruyoga of the dynamic Vajrasattva as the sole door of entry to real practice for those of virtuous inclination. Firstly, carry out the general preliminaries, beginning with taking refuge and generating the bodhi-mind:)

I take refuge in the Buddha, I take refuge in the Teachings and I take refuge in the Spiritual Community until I gain enlightenment. By the virtue I gather from practicing giving and the other perfections, may I attain Buddhahood in order to benefit all beings. (3X)

(Then contemplate the four immeasurables:)

May all beings be endowed with happiness.
May all beings be free of suffering.
May all beings never be separated from happiness.
May all beings abide in equanimity undisturbed by the
  eight worldly attitudes or by dualistic preconceptions.

(The actual practice commences with the incantation of the formula to correct one's mental perception:)

OṂ SVABHĀVA SHUDHAḤ SARVA DHARMĀḤ
SVABHĀVA SHUDDHO 'HAṂ

By nature everything is emptiness.
Within the sphere of emptiness, which is without origin
  or end,
At the crown of my head on a lion-supported throne,
Appears the symbol PAṂ which becomes a white lotus.

Upon it is the syllable ĀḤ which becomes a moon disc.
Upon that, in the nature of bliss and emptiness, is a white syllable HŪṂ
Which becomes the mighty and glorious Vajrasattva
One with my root Master, who is the epitome of all refuge.
The Master is in color flawless conch-white crystal
With a perceptive sublimity unerringly encompassing all beings;
He has one face and two hands holding vajra and bell.
His two feet are locked in an immovable full lotus posture.
On his lap is the consort Adamantine Pride who is white in color
Holding a curved knife and skull-cup, her legs encircling his body.
They revel in the embrace of exhilarating great bliss,
Are clad in celestial raiment and wear the eight precious ornaments;
Transparent light diffuses from their bodies, and although
Insubstantial like a rainbow, this light fills infinite realms.
At the crown, throat and heart are the three immutable deities
In the aspect of white, red and blue syllables respectively.
Light radiates from the heart, inviting all the Victorious Ones;
JAḤ HŪṂ BAṂ HOḤ—they merge into the pair and become inseparably one.

(The seven-limb offering:)

I prostrate to you, my supreme exalted Master,
The active personification of the Tathagatas of the three times,
The Protector possessing the great unification of method and wisdom.
Which is a remarkable mandala of innate bliss and the void,
Exactly like the pervasion of space within itself.

The infinitude of your single-pointed concentration on the bliss and the void
Yields captivating rainbow-hued offering goddesses of tender years.

May they delight the entire assembly of the myriad Victorious Ones
Through a host of auspicious offerings granting all possible bliss.

OṂ VAJRA SAPARIVARA ARGHAṂ (and so on till SHABDA) PRATĪCHCHHA HŪṂ SVĀHĀ.

Furthermore, may I offer with peerless enthusiasm
The quintessence of the world and beyond
As well as endless excellent offerings both actual and imagined—
The entirety in their outer, inner, secret and suchness forms.

I see that the result of my negativities and downfalls,
Which I have accumulated since beginningless time,
Will be but fuel for my burning in the hell without respite;
Hence I regret them as if I had taken poison,
And resolve to maintain further scrupulous restraint;
Thus I admit and confess all my multitude of faults.

I rejoice in the cultivation of all wholesome activity,
Not merely my own but I also take pleasure
In the superlative meritorious endeavors
Of ordinary beings, Superiors and Conquerors,
According to their respective capacities in virtuous work.

As the chronicles tell of great Brahma's offering to Shakyamuni,
An enormous wheel with one thousand spokes—all of perfect gold,
So I entreat all Masters to teach the noble Doctrine uninterruptedly,
Thus opening the door to the excellent path bringing everlasting joy.

The Enjoyment Body of the Protector manifests appearance
Which, in the guise of Emanation Bodies accords with conventional forms.
May you all steadily continue your sublime work of the three doors
Which equals in number the particles of myriad worlds.

I dedicate not only the virtuous power accumulated by
my own modest endeavors,
But also the ocean-like immensity of others' merit,
That limitless sentient beings may pass beyond transitory
woes
And gain the ineffable jewel of peerless enlightenment.

(Requests:)

This life resembles an ephemeral autumn cloud,
Grasping at it ensnares one in the eight worldly attitudes;
So please, out of your compassion, protect this great fool
Who tastes honey-nectar tainted by the canker of worldly
opulence.

Please bless me to travel the excellent path
Of the causal and resultant Tantric Vehicle,
Thereby speedily achieving perfect enlightenment
So that I may free all tormented sentient beings
Who are incessantly plagued by the infernal succession
of suffering's round.

My past indulgence in one hundred shortcomings of the
three doors
Has resulted in evil action which now bears fruit
In an array of erroneous and hideous appearances,
Like the terrifying potents of the callous Lord of Death.
Upon their arrival, to whom can I turn?

Bemoaning my plight for such reasons as these,
I seek refuge in the Master, a fountain of compassion,
And in the Triple Gem from this very moment on.
Please enable me to purify my host of black actions
By means of confession and future unfailing restraint,
Even should that require the cost of my life.

Following these requests, there then appears around
The HUM of the moon disc at the heart of the Father and
Mother,
The one hundred syllable mantra resembling a necklace
of pearls,
From which light radiates into the ten directions.
The rays become offerings to all the Victorious Ones,
Thus further enhancing the rays' magnificence.

This mass of brilliant light returns and dissolves
Into the syllables of the mantra rosary,
Producing a flawless and potent nectar
Which gushes and cascades down into the crown
Apertures of myself and all other sentient beings;
It cleanses every trace of defilement, and thus
We are imbued with all power, energy and excellence.

(Now recite the mantra whilst maintaining an awareness of the four opponent powers and their purpose, as well as avoiding any lapse in concentration on the visualization:)

OM VAJRASATTVA SAMAYA, MANU PALAYA, VAJRASATTVA TVENO PATISHTHA, DRIDHO ME BHAVA, SUPOSHYO ME BHAVA, SUTOSHYO ME BHAVA, ANURAKTO ME BHAVA, SARVA SIDDHIM ME PRAYACHCHHA, SARVA KARMA SUCHA ME, CHITTAM SHRIYAM KHURU HUM, HA HA HA HA HOH BHAGAVAN, SARVA TATHAGATA, VAJRA MA ME MUNCHA, VAJRA BHAVA, MAHA SAMAYA SATTVA AH HUM PHAT.

(To conclude the session:)

Due to ignorance and bewilderment,
I have transgressed and degenerated my words of honor.
I take refuge in you, the foremost Vajra-holder,
Lord of all sentient beings,
An embodiment of great compassion.

By dint of my entreaties to this paragon of excellence,
My Master restores me to a wholesome condition.
Thereafter the Father and Mother, from the crown of their heads down,
Merge gradually into the eight branch psychic channels
Which fan out from the heart of the Father, Vajrasattva.
The channels dissolve into the lotus above them,
Which in turn fades away into the moon.
The moon disc dissolves into the mantra rosary
Which then fades into the syllable HUM,
And HUM becomes immutably
The indelible nature of my mind.

The colophon: This method of Guruyoga practice for purification of negativities, utilizing the inseparability of the Spiritual Master and Vajrasattva, was composed by the fully ordained Buddhist monk Losang Kalsang Gyatso in the Potala Palace at the insistence of the steward Kunga Chodan, who desired a daily meditation practice.

Translated by Kevin Garratt with Chomdze Tashi Wangyal.

Source References

Dalai Lama I:

gSung-'bum-thor-bu, "Miscellaneous Writings," Collected Works, Vol. VI, Tashi Lhunpo Edition.

Dalai Lama II:

Yid-dam-sgrub-skor, "Concerning the Meditational Deity, Practices," Collected Works, Vol. II, Drepung Edition.

Dalai Lama V:

Lha-tshogs-rnams-kyi-sgrub-skor, "Concerning the Methods of Accomplishing the Various Deities," Collected Works, Vol. III, Bhutan Edition.

Dalai Lama VII:

dBang-dang-rjes-gnang-sogs-kyi-sngon-gro, "The Preliminaries of Receiving the Empowerments and Initiations," Collected Works, Vol. II. Drepung Edition.

Lha-mang-sgrub-skor, "Concerning the Accomplishment of the Deity Methods," Collected Works, Vol. IV.

Bla-ma'i rnal-'byor-gyi-rim-pa-phyogs-gcig-tu-bkod-pa, "A Collection of Guru Methods," Collected Works, Vol. IV.

Dalai Lama XIII:

Lha-tsogs-sgrub-skor, "Concerning the Accomplishment of Various Deities," Collected Works, Vol. V, Potala Edition.

Note on the Sanskrit

Sanskrit is a complex language, with fifty-two letters; the only way to accurately transliterate all these letters into the Roman system—that used in English—is to use diacritic marks. Although this method creates headaches for both the writer and the printer, it is worth pursuing in the case of the tantras because an inaccurate transliteration of a mantra will weaken its power.

The Tibetan alphabet has only thirty letters. Thus Tibetan shares the same problem with English. The Tibetan system of transliterating Sanskrit does not use diacritics; the Tibetans use mirror images of some letters, and stack other letters on top of each other. But the result is the same as the diacritic system—a big headache for the printer. Hence, many transliterations of Sanskrit mantras and words are corrupt in Tibetan books, and one can often find many different spellings of the same mantra. Finding the original spelling is a tiresome chore.

We have done our best to spell the mantras correctly, although mistakes have no doubt escaped our notice. The actual system of translation we have adopted is the one used by Professor Jeffrey Hopkins in his books. It has the advantage of being the easiest system for the neophyte to pronounce with reasonable accuracy.

Note that the Tibetans themselves developed an eclectic system of pronouncing Sanskrit words that would make a pandit wince; Westerners, therefore, need not be embarrassed by their faulty pronunciation. Some translations of tantra published in the West attempt to write the matters in the Tibetan pronunciation. This only leads to confusion. It is much better to go back to the source: Sanskrit. Also, because the Tibetans visualize the syllables in Tibetan spelling, there is no reason why westerners cannot visualize them in their own script.